ISBN 9781036934163

First Edition: 2025

Cover design by: Claire Pepper

Illustrations by: Claire Pepper

Publisher: Beacons and Horizons Publishing.

www.weatheringcancersstorm.com

This book is based on real-life experiences. While every effort has been made to reflect the emotional truth of the journey, identifying details and names may have been changed to protect the privacy of individuals.

This book is not intended to act as a replacement for medical advice, treatment plans or clinical support. Its intention is to act as a companion – not a prescription.

A copy of this publication is to be submitted to the British Library under legal deposit.

FREE PRINTABLE RESOURCES.

The intention behind the book is to provide support for people who are watching a child they love fight against cancer, and this would be incomplete without providing you with a link for free printable resources.

These resources include a medication tracker, a prescription tracker, a hospital packing list and more. Adding free resources is something I try to do regularly and is based upon challenges that my family and I have encountered throughout my son's cancer journey.

These resources can be found, downloaded, and printed at home by going to our website: *www.weatheringcancersstorm.com*

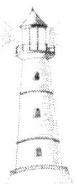

For Jacob. My captain, my compass, my beacon. It's easy to stay the course when we have you at the helm of our boat. To Imogen, Charlie and Mark, my crewmates, and the reason I keep going, I'm so lucky to have you beside me as we weather this storm together.

Now… bring me that horizon.

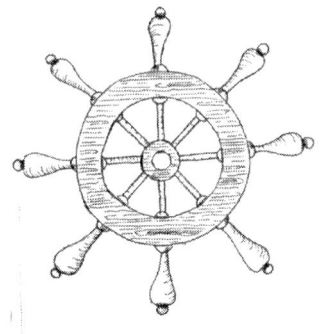

FOREWORD

By Tim Sadler

Dad to Michael, Author, Illustrator, Fellow educator,

and Founder of Mind the Chaps.

I first came across Claire Pepper when she commented on a video I made for the Department for Health and Social Care with my son Michael. Young Lives vs Cancer, a charity I volunteer for, asked us to film a short video detailing Michael's diagnosis in 2014 with Acute Lymphoblastic Leukaemia. The video was shared widely, and Michael received so much love for telling his story. I reached to out Claire after her kind words and I'm so glad I did.

Any cancer diagnosis is devastating, but nothing can prepare you for learning it's your own child. When Michael was diagnosed, it felt like my heart had been ripped out of my chest. He was only two years old; how on earth could my son have cancer?

I thought my family had already been through enough after my sister, Katie, was diagnosed with and sadly died from Neuroblastoma in October 2000. I was a teenager at the time and did not cope well. I hid behind humour and buried my head in the sand. I didn't know what was happening to my sister and I think I was too scared to truly appreciate the severity of her condition at the time. After the sad loss of my sister, I could never have contemplated that cancer could tap me on the shoulder again and turn my world upside down. But it did, and once again, it was someone I love being harmed.

There's no right or wrong way to handle the news of a family member with a cancer diagnosis. Equally there's no right or wrong way to act as a result, but there are some ways that are probably more right than others. As a parent, you know that searching the internet for reassurances is dangerous but when you're desperate, you'll cling on to anything. I tried to keep my head above water for my family's sake, but I was struggling to come to terms with my son's diagnosis, and I felt like I was drowning.

It's hard enough to reason with a person you know and love, but it's harder to explain to a nearly three-year-old as to why people are prodding him, stabbing him, and giving him cocktails that make him feel hideous, even though they are supposed to be making him better. Family situations vary and I became the default 'restrainer' as I was the only one that could hold Michael long enough for the doctors and nurses to administer the treatment he needed to progress. Combined with steroids that severely affected his mood, Michael was fearful to be near me and almost didn't speak to me for the best part of six months. I wasn't 'Dad' to him during that period; I was the nasty person who had to wrestle him until he was too tired to move, just so they could give him an injection. I was incredibly anxious and depressed as a result and I felt so powerless at the time. Claire refers to stormy seas and facing the trials and tribulations involved after a cancer diagnosis. You feel like you're up a certain creek without a paddle and weathering that storm seems impossible. Whoever you are and whatever your belief system or background, we all look for reassurances - a ray of light, whether natural or created by humans. As I've learnt more about Claire and the work, she has been doing to provide guidance and support for families with a child being treated for cancer, I see more and more how she's creating answers for difficult questions. I wish I had some of the amazing lighthouse resources to use and refer to during Michael's cancer journey.

As I write this, on 24th June 2025 it is 8 years to the day since Michael rang the bell to signal the end of his treatment. It would also have been my sister's 46th birthday if she were still alive. The dates lining up is just a coincidence but it's a bittersweet one. It reminds me of how grateful I should be that Michael is now a happy and healthy 14yearold, who starts his GCSEs in September. It also reminds me that so many families don't get to see their child finish their journey. My parents lost their daughter and my brother, and I lost our sister. I use the term 'lost' as many families struggle to find the right words to explain why someone in their life is missing. However, the journey ends, finding a post-treatment purpose or reason for being is crucial.

After Michael finished his treatment, and along with Young Lives vs Cancer, I helped to set up the 'Mind the Chaps' network. A group specifically created to support fathers of the oncology wards. Mums and Dads equally deserve support, but let's be honest, men often need the proverbial 'kick up the arse' to something about it and seek help when it they need it. Early intervention is the key.

Claire also believes in helping families sooner, and whether it's her Lighthouse Emergency Support Kit (for noting down blood results and medication doses) or the fun activity books to keep little hands busy on the wards, there is something for everyone in the same boat, as we all furiously try to paddle against the current.

It warms my heart to learn about Claire's work in helping other families, despite her own impossibly difficult circumstances. Her strength to turn such a heart-breaking negative into a positive for others is inspiring to say the least. Claire cares about the whole family and understands the difficulty in negotiating the turbulent waters of supporting a child with cancer. She sees it as a voyage that is easier to attempt when you are not alone. Trying to find calm during chaotic times is hard but Claire's mission seems to be asking herself about the practical steps families can take. What can they change about their situation? What do they have no control over? How can I help?

I could've done with a lighthouse, with a Claire Pepper over a decade ago to hold my hand and light the way a little. Her determination to help others despite her own hard times is truly an inspiration and I'm honoured to have been asked to write the foreword to this book.

Thank you, Claire. X

Table of Contents

FREE PRINTABLE RESOURCES.................................2

FOREWORD...4

INTRODUCTION...13

THE CLOUDS GATHER – CANCER? NOW WHAT?..15

THE FIRST RUMBLE OF THUNDER — ZERO TO SIXTY IN TEN SECONDS............................21

JACOB'S STORY..28

GALE FORCE WINDS – WHEN WORDS FAIL: TALKING TO YOUR CHILD ABOUT THE IMPOSSIBLE..32

THE TEMPEST – CHEMO AND JOINING THE HAIR LOSS CLUB. 38

FREDDIE'S STORY 49

THE EYE OF THE STORM — THE CANCER BUBBLE AND VENTURING OUTSIDE OF IT. 55

NAVIGATING ROUGH SEAS — HOSPITAL STAYS AND SURGICAL PROCEDURES. 62

WORDS FROM OUR ONCOLOGIST. 72

THE UNSEEN WAVES — RADIOTHERAPY ... CUE THE GLOW IN THE DARK JOKES. 78

THE LIFEBOAT – SIBLINGS: THE FORGOTTEN SUPERHEROES. 87

MENTAL HEALTH ADVICE FROM A COUNSELLOR. 93

TRYING NOT TO CAPCIZE – CAREGIVER BURNOUT: FILLING THE CUPS OF OTHERS WHEN YOURS IS EMPTY. 101

LOST AT SEA — MANAGING MENTAL HEALTH: UNTANGLING A BALL OF STRING.....................107

PAIN INTO PURPOSE: PARENTS WITH THE HEARTS OF LIONS. 113

THE AFTERMATH OF THE STORM — REMISSION… GETTING ON WITH 'IT'. 124

THE BEACON OF LIGHT — CANCER CHARITIES
AND SUPPORT; IT'S OKAY TO ASK FOR HELP.130

CLOSING STATEMENT BY DR. ANISHA PATEL,
GP..141

AUTHORS NOTE. 143

SPECIAL THANKS....................................145

JOIN THE CONVERSATION 148

INTRODUCTION

Chances are, you have bought this book because you or someone you know has a child who has been diagnosed with Cancer. If that is the case, I am so sorry. Your child deserved better than the hand they have been dealt, and so did you. This is the book I know other parents like me need, but I wish they didn't.

Now that you have been involuntarily enrolled in the 'Parents of Children with Cancer Club', your free, lifetime membership has thrust you into an alien territory that is scarcely talked about in the public domain. The reality is that it's just too awful and too sad. No one in this club ever imagined or ever wanted to be enrolled. None of us want the 'my child has cancer' t-shirt or keyring. Yet here we are. This new, uncharted landscape has no map. There is no satnav to guide you through. I often think it's like playing a never-ending game of snakes and ladders … blindfolded, and where the board and the rules of the game are constantly changing.

When my son was diagnosed at 12 years old with Mesenchymal Chondrosarcoma, a rare and aggressive form of Bone Cancer, I tried to turn to my love of books for insight, and I found that there weren't any that offered me what I needed… guidance and advice for the entire journey. So, I had to do what everyone else has done before me and develop my own sense of direction before I could even begin to think about how I was going to lead my family through this. This is an unnecessary additional pressure on you as a parent that I hope this book helps to alleviate. I won't be able to offer you a magic solution, or step-by-step instructions. But I can help you learn to navigate this storm through highlighting things I felt blindsided by and things that helped my family and I through the pages of this book which are based on my own experience born insight.

So, when you feel like the waves are hitting harder than you ever imagined, when you're drowning in fear, exhaustion, and uncertainty – look for the beacon of light that I hope to have weaved into the pages of this book. It is there to remind you that you are not alone in this storm. You may feel that way sometimes, but I promise you it isn't true.

THE CLOUDS GATHER – CANCER? NOW WHAT?

"I am not afraid of storms, for I am learning how to sail

my ship."

Louisa May Alcott

I don't expect you have the time or the emotional energy reserves for me to ease you into this; after all, cancer isn't easing you in gently is it? So, if it's okay with you, we are going to hit the ground running. Firstly, there are no right or wrong ways to deal with a receiving a Cancer diagnosis. It isn't always an automatic case of getting straight on the phone to Make a Wish, starting a GoFundMe page and getting your child to write a bucket list. Whilst I do always advocate for reaching out to charities and having discussions about the situation with your child as good starting points, the most important thing to remember is that aside from how you initially take the news, a diagnosis leads to treatment. This means that even though they are unable to offer you any iron clad guarantees, clinicians will always 'treat to cure' and if there are treatment options available, there are reasons to be positive. However, as positivity and speaking with your child about their cancer journey are vital steps in this fight, we will cover them in more detail in later chapters.

What may come as an initial shock to you is the fact that your worst nightmare is now your reality. The reason why it this is, is because it is such a tragic and upsetting subject, and most people don't let it linger in their brains for very long let alone talk about it. I was one of them. I would say "that's such a shame" and then shake the topic out of my head. Not acknowledging cancer before this point does not make you a bad person, it makes you human. Sometimes life is so dark and cruel that we simply cannot comprehend it. So, we don't ... not until we have no alternative. But it is a very dark, terrifying and disorienting place to live once you find it has become your new reality.

Once your child receives a diagnosis, you may struggle with the way your life appears to feel different to how it was 24 hours before. Almost like when a loved one passes away, our life often feels like an out of body experience. That was how I felt for a long time after my son's diagnosis. I fell asleep with the mantra that he would be okay and woke feeling like I was in someone else's body every day for at least the first year. This is okay. I always say that change isn't everyone's cup of tea, because not everyone likes tea. So, to have our lives as a family and my own as a parent change so drastically in such a short space of time, it was a lot for me to wrap my head around. I want to let you know here that there is no right or wrong way to process what's going on. Do what you feel is right for you but just make sure that you keep moving forward. One step at a time, one day at a time. Even if it's celebrating the little wins that help you feel like you are still in control, like "I actually showered today!" or "I actually had something to eat!" believe me, I know only too well what an achievement those can be on the rough days.

I found I went through the grieving process, which came as a complete surprise. Initially it was like being hit with a wall of shock, followed by denial. Then I went into fear and anger before I finally moved towards acceptance. However, as the process unfolds, you may find yourself moving backwards and forwards through the stages. The most important thing is to remember that there is no instruction manual for life and if there were, this wouldn't even feature in the troubleshooting section at the back. There are no rules for when this happens and when it does, all bets are off. There is no normal, so be patient with yourself and know that you are not alone. Not by a long shot. As a mother who's son is 3 years into a battle he won't win, advice is this: firstly, comparison is said to be the theft of joy, and this couldn't be any truer for Cancer. Cancer isn't a cookie cutter illness. It doesn't look the way it is depicted on the television. You cannot compare your situation to those of others; it is unique just as your child is. What could take one individual many years to achieve remission, others could take a year or take the form of being held hostage by years of scans. It is like comparing apples to oranges. Additionally, remain focused on facts and only the stage that lies ahead of you. Do not allow the demons of 'what might be' or "what you could have done differently" to begin banging on your door. If it isn't happening right now, park it and come back to it when it is in the present. If it's in the past and you can't change it? Let it go. Do not go down the path of what might be. Because that road is a really long road to nowhere. When my child was initially diagnosed, Queen Elizabeth II had just died and seeing the death of such a massive public figure messed with my head. It brought up a whole world of what might be and what could happen. Do not go down that path. Focus on what is happening right now. There is peace to be found in facts and in the present.

Finally, you will be tempted to start looking for reasons why your child has cancer. Stop! There are none. No, it isn't fair, no it hasn't been sent as a punishment for your past, no you did not wrong someone in a past life and there are no answers for why it wasn't you instead.

Those were the questions I asked myself, the universe, and anyone willing to listen and I must level with you, no one will have the answers to those kinds of questions. Not even the doctors could offer me reasons why my child had the type of cancer he was diagnosed with. It was explained to me as "just bad luck." But what I did eventually come to realise is that the cruel irony behind Cancer is it doesn't discriminate, it is the only thing on our planet that doesn't. It doesn't see race, gender, social class, age, background, religion, political affiliations, or sexual orientation. There is no easier way to put it other than it is what it is, there is no justice or reasoning behind its unwelcome arrival in your life. I wish someone had given me this advice; I struggled with finding the logic behind why any individual is still suffering at the hands of this relentless and cold-hearted killer. This felt especially cruel when technology enables us to have so much and yet, it cannot do the one thing we need; save our loved one's lives. So, I urge you to listen to my advice and save yourself some time and the inevitable heartache that follows by resisting the urge to look for reasons why this is happening to your child and to your family.

Receiving the news that your precious child has cancer puts the world you have built through the shredder. However, what you must do… and this next step is crucial… you must now make a conscious decision about how you are going to deal with it. How are you going to lead your family through it? How are you going to keep moving forwards both as an individual and as a parent? It's like the saying goes, it's not what happens to you that defines you, it's how you deal with it… and that's my reason for writing this book. I found myself in alien territory, and it is a subject no one really wants to talk about, so there aren't many books to give you any kind of insight, especially not from a parent's perspective. Yes, this is an indescribably horrendous situation. No, you and your family don't deserve this. But you also don't deserve to be in this storm without a map and without any kind of support. So, I am going to be your lighthouse until you are ready to become one yourself. Until then, we are going to navigate this storm together.

THE FIRST RUMBLE OF THUNDER — ZERO TO SIXTY IN TEN SECONDS

"There are some things you learn best in calm, and some

in storm."

Willa Cather

Okay, so your gut was right and there *was* something wrong with your child, life threateningly wrong. But now what? I hope the title gives you a little clue. I admit, it did make me smile. Only because it is exactly how it felt for me as a parent after receiving my own child's diagnosis. I have never received so many phone calls and appointment letters in such a short space of time before and quite honestly, it made my head spin. So, ensure you get yourself a notepad and a pen, then keep it close by...

because you're going to need it. Lots of people are now going to want to see your child and you're the gatekeeper.

The problem with this is that sometimes individuals that work in medicine forget that you are not a colleague and you do not speak their lingo. Don't not be afraid to remind them to talk to you in plain English. Expect to hear from your oncologist, the radiology team, and your support team. This is where appointments will be scheduled to talk to you more about treatment plans and what kind of support they can offer you. For some, this is where biopsies are scheduled and for others these appointments will appear because of a biopsy. What you need to find comfort in now is that the more they investigate into the cancer, the more they understand. The more they understand, the better they can treat it.

Ironically, with the rush of people trying to gain access to your child through you, be prepared for the lulls that come between. Where your life seems to turn into suspended animation whilst the powers that be hold countless meetings to interpret results and decide on how best to proceed. I want to be real with you for a second, this can take weeks. These weeks can feel agonizing as you wait for updates. They are usually called multi-disciplinary meetings. Basically, it's where everyone involved in your child's medical care will meet, potentially look at scans and decide how best to move forward. It's hard being at the bottom of the pile but the reality is that you will be the last to know. Be prepared for that.

For me, we were told a biopsy was merely a formality. In the end he had two painful biopsies almost two months apart so that they could specifically identify and diagnose the type of cancer my child had. Most of this time involved waiting around for someone to contact us and give us the low down on exactly what was holding my child hostage, then more waiting whilst they decided how best to treat it. The important thing to remember is that the waits that come in between appointments are there because practitioners and medical professionals want to be as certain as they can about what it is and most importantly, what they are going to do about it. As frustrating as it will feel for you, this is not something to jump into with only half the facts.

My advice would be; if there is something you do not understand, say so. If there is a question you feel is taboo and aren't sure whether to ask or not, take a deep breath and spit it out. No one is going to ask for you, no one is going to judge you for asking and if you don't, you will never get an answer. Albeit there are no guarantees that there will be answers but it if you don't, the question will continue to rattle around in your head. There is nothing these professionals haven't heard before, especially the questions that are harder to ask. I found I only had one question. I knew I wasn't the only one thinking it, but I also knew that no one else was brave enough to ask. So, I asked it; "is my child going to die?" No one you pose that question to will have the response you are looking for, but they will all share the same passion and drive to cure your child, even if they don't verbalise it to you. If you take nothing else away from this book, please take that. Once you are told what type of cancer your child has, you will be drawn towards googling it. The best piece of advice I ever received was from a friend whose son survived cancer. She made me promise to never google anything to do with my sons' cancer. She was right. I promise you, no good will come of doing that. I know as humans we are driven towards learning about things that we don't understand but you will only find facts and figures that will have you sobbing uncontrollably. Not only will no one be able to comfort you afterwards, but you won't be able to forget what you have read. Her advice was to elect someone, preferably someone who has been in your shoes, to be your researcher. Give them a question you want answering and leave it with them. However, please don't fly off the handle if they say they can't google the answer, especially if it is on survival rates. Because the next question you will ask yourself is which bracket will your child fit in? The survival rate or the death rate. No one will, not even google can tell you that. Nothing good ever comes from googling cancer.

Also, brace yourself for the fact that you will now be hypersensitive to anything related to cancer. My husband and I found that when we turned to tv to 'switch off' from the situation we now found ourselves in, cancer was everywhere. Every tv plot line, every other advert; people looking for a cure, people with no hair and looking sick, and people saying they were in remission. It has developed into a weird source of amusement for us. When a plotline is developing, one of us will say "I'll bet it's cancer" or when a character reveals their diagnosis to a loved one, our response will usually be "of course it is. Of course, it's cancer." Brace yourselves for that. There was one instance recently where the episode of a tv show included a person who had a child with cancer, it was in the same part of the body, they had the same name, and they had the same prognosis. Our response was "Full house!". My

point is that it will feel like it's everywhere you look. Whilst it is easy to get angry at not being able to escape your new reality, try to bear in mind that by keeping it in the public eye, it continues to encourage society to pursue a cure, even if that won't be an immediate reality for us. However, if you feel like it is raising your blood pressure and your anxiety beyond tolerable levels, try leaning on your comfort tv shows. If you are like me, you know most of them word for word and therefore won't be blindsided by an unexpected storyline. You are human, this is unimaginably hard, and you can only cope with what you can cope with, so play to your own interests and existing movie and tv knowledge to steer you clear of regular tv if you find it's a trigger for you.

I found turning to my favourite movies and tv shows were easy ways to distract myself whilst I waited for medical teams to come back to me because of how long it can take for people to get back to you. For me, it felt a lot to me like I had taken an exam, and my life was on pause. It will be hard to endure in the beginning, the silence gets loud sometimes, but it won't always feel alien to you. Three years in, I have got used to the lull between appointments. I find that life feels a lot like it did before my child's diagnosis and I tend to forget that our lives are in fact anything but normal. Something will happen such as needing medication to mitigate the side effects being caused by another type of medication which will snap me out of my parental autopilot, and I will switch into 'cancer mum mode'. Its second nature now. Both roles co-exist now and run parallel depending on the setting I am in. At work, I can exist without cancer dictating everything. At home, I run, I cook, I laugh. Then when an appointment comes around, cancer mum takes the steering wheel. It all happens without much active thought these days.

With time, you will eventually turn your focus on the ever-increasing to-do list that has been growing whilst you have been adjusting to being a parent of a child with cancer. Ticking things off this list whilst you wait can give you back a sense of control that you may feel that you lost. Comfort can be found in the fact that some things have stayed the same. Okay, it may be doing the weekly shop, taking another child to an extra-curricular activity, or doing the school run.

As mundane as they are, they have stayed the same and they are things you remain in control of. You can find some version of normal if you look hard enough. It will seem impossible at first and that is both understandable and completely normal. I want you to know that just like seeing the beacon of a lighthouse standing steadfast on a cliff during a dark and stormy night, there will be some version of normality waiting for you when you are ready to look for it.

JACOB'S STORY

It is September 2022 and for the last year, 12-year-old Jacob has had a lump on his pelvis that has been getting bigger for over a year. Doctors have said several times that the lump was being caused by puberty. However, Jacob encountered some mobility issues during a family holiday abroad that his mum couldn't ignore. As a result, she took him to accident and emergency at the local hospital when they returned home. It was here that his mum was told that the most likely cause of the pain was cancer.

Jacob has a rare and aggressive form of Bone Cancer called Mesenchymal Chondrosarcoma. It is unresponsive to Chemotherapy, Radiotherapy, and there are only 800 known cases of this type of cancer in medical history. Jacob had several rounds of chemotherapy to try and shrink the tumour. Unfortunately, the chemotherapy was unsuccessful, and Jacob's entire left leg was amputated because surgical removal is the only known method of successful treatment for this type of cancer. This should have been a devastating blow for Jacob. However, he retained his fierce determination, and the sheer will he possessed to push through any obstacles. Losing a physical part of his body should have left Jacob questioning his identity. After all, it holds the potential to completely break a person. However, twenty-four hours after having his leg taken, Jacob was asking the medical staff for the overhead bars and within forty-eight hours, Jacob was being told off by nurses for doing pull ups on them. Fast forward a few months and after recovering from this, he spent 8 weeks in

Manchester being treated with Proton Beam radiotherapy at The Christie Hospital. Once this was completed, Jacob and his family were told he would have quarterly scans for at least the next five years because this type of cancer has a high relapse rate.

In September 2023, Jacob's parents were told that a piece of the tumour has broken off during his amputation surgery months before and had now settled in his lungs. There are now between 30 and 40 known tumours in Jacob's lungs and surgical removal is not an option this time.

Because there are not enough patients battling this cancer, there are insufficient numbers to hold medical trials for medical solutions. So, Jacob is now on medication called 'Cancer blockers.' This medication blocks the growth signal from the brain to the cancer cells in the hope that it slows down the rate that they multiply and slows the rate of growth. The aim of this is to buys both him and his family some invaluable time. He is currently stable and has been for over two years.

Throughout it all, Jacob has handled every blow that cancer has dealt him with the same unshakable determination and optimism. He is now a part of the England Amputee Football Association; he has been to several premier league football stadiums and met a significant amount of premier league football players. He has learned to ski, learned to swim for the second time in his life, raced supercars, completed an indoor sky dive and many other experiences. As his mum, he has shown me that even though I thought I would be swallowed by the darkness forever, he was my beacon when I needed one. His battle with cancer won't be a success story. However, he is a prime example of how cancer can back you into a corner, where it holds the potential to hold you hostage for the rest of your days and you still hold the power to fight back with a steadfast determination to make the time you have left the best it can possibly be.

I may have built the lighthouse, but he has always been the beacon, and it is a privilege to be the one he calls "mum."

GALE FORCE WINDS – WHEN WORDS FAIL: TALKING TO YOUR CHILD ABOUT THE IMPOSSIBLE.

"Life's roughest storms prove the strength of our anchors."

Unknown.

When we were first told my son had cancer, he had just been for his MRI. His dad and I were in a little side room and my son was tucking into some chicken nuggets, chips and beans in another. They said that they will need to take a biopsy of the tumour, so we asked if they would tell us afterwards if it was malignant or benign. We were then hit with the revelation that a biopsy was merely a formality, and they knew it was cancer already. It was in that moment that whilst the ground was crumbling beneath me that I mustered up all my courage and asked, "is my child going to die?" That's the first thing that ran through my mind, the sheer undiluted terror caused by the possibility of losing something so precious to me. So, I reached out for reassurance, but in cancer's world there are no iron clad guarantees. Their response was that they will do everything they can to make sure he doesn't die. Then it struck me like a ten-tonne truck… how on earth am I going to tell my child? This is one of the hardest conversations a parent will ever have with their child and its one that you don't get a script for. The reality for me was that I knew as soon as we told him, the childlike innocence would drain from his eyes, and he would grow up in a heartbeat. That's the bit they don't talk about in the media, how our children lose their childhood and their entire identity as soon as they hear the phrase "you've got cancer" and the truth is, you will also mourn for who you were and the world you were a part of before you heard those dreaded and unforgettable words that will be etched in your memory forever. You feel so helpless as a parent because there is no way to shield them from what they are going to face, and there are no words to make it better. Your heart will be breaking, but you have to summon up all the strength you possess to remain strong for them. It is okay to feel like you want to have all the answers, to say that it's going to be okay, but you also need to brace yourself for the fact that you can't offer any false promises just to try and minimise the heartache.

This is most likely to race through your mind at lightning speed. You've been delivered the hardest piece of news that you will ever receive as a parent and you're still trying to wrap your head around it yourself. Now you realise that you also have to tell your child. I know I'm not about to give you a step-by-step guide on how to break the news, but I hope that by providing you with my own perspective and experience, it will help you feel more equipped to handle it as best you can. Because that is all you can do... your best.

You know your child better than anyone. Some children will know something's wrong, and they will want to openly discuss it, ask you questions or pump you for information like a detective on a tv crime drama. Others will say absolutely nothing and appear to shut it out completely. My child was the latter. Because he was a tweenager at the time, we were able to be a little more open and honest about the situation. But try to remind yourself of just how observant children actually are because this will help you to enter the situation with both eyes open. In the beginning, we had told him that the biopsies were investigative procedures aiming to find out what exactly was wrong. This was because we wanted to let him be a child for as long as we possibly could. Then we would have a treatment plan in place so that when we did tell him it was cancer, we could also tell him what the medical team were planning to do about it. However, during this time he had pieced things together and when we came to discuss it with him, it was more a case of confirming what he already knew. In our situation, this made the conversation easier for us as parents and for him as our child. By doing it this way we were able to have a straightforward conversation discussing the facts rather that giving him hopes and maybes. We wanted him to be able to focus on what was happening in that moment, because the reality was that none of us knew what the future held. Months passed by without him discussing it. He just pushed it to one side and carried on with life and from our perspective, these were valuable additional months of normality before the inevitable and permanent shift finally arrived. However, one day, three months after being diagnosed, whilst sitting on the stairs waiting for a taxi to take him to hospital for an appointment, he came out with "well if I'm going to die, I'm going to die". It was in that moment that I realised that despite giving the impression that he wasn't dealing with it, that he was ignoring it completely, he had in fact been processing it in his way and on his terms. He had already come to accept the potential fate of losing his battle and I was in awe of how he was able to accept something I couldn't, and still can't.

No matter what happens, you are the person who knows your child better than anyone else on earth. You know their temperament and personality. This knowledge will form the backbone of how you decide it best to deliver the news. However, this doesn't need to be straight away. Take a beat, try and wrap your head around it before you jump straight into having this discussion. This is the moment where everything changes. There are no second chances at having this conversation and if you're not in the right headspace for it, you are going to potentially forget information, and the underlying message of reassurance that you want to deliver is going to be jumbled up and lost. So, it's a case of getting the balance right between taking time to get your head around it and not extending the waiting period out for too long so that it becomes the elephant in the room. I would recommend talking to your oncologist and the cancer nurses about how to break the news. The sad reality of the situation is that they do this all the time. They have had this conversation with parents and their children countless times, use their expertise. For us, we waited until we were at a check-up appointment, we had notified our oncologist and the cancer nurses in advance to make sure that they were in the room with us, and we discussed it with medical experts and pastoral support. That way if we missed anything out, if we got any information wrong or we were approaching the conversation from the wrong angle, they would be there to steer the conversation back to where it needed to go. When you do decide to have this conversation, be prepared to be asked questions that you don't know the answer to and you need to get used to feeling okay with saying "I don't know." I used to partner that response with "I'll write it down and we can ask the oncologist when we see him next." Stay away from medical terminology, keep it honest, simple and to the point. Focus on the facts, those are going to keep you on the right track. The best thing you can do in this situation is say that they aren't alone, that you are going to be by their side throughout their entire battle, and that you and the medical team will everything possible to make them better. Because that is the truth. Throughout their life, you have known that you would move heaven and earth for your child, and that has not changed. You may not have chosen to be in the middle of the storm that cancer is unleashing on you and your family, but now you know you can't run from it. The only choice you have is to decide how you are going to face it. Are you going to be swallowed by the waves or are you going to focus on that lighthouse and keep going?

THE TEMPEST – CHEMO AND JOINING THE HAIR LOSS CLUB.

"Storms draw something out of us that calm seas don't."

Bill Hybels.

This is probably the aspect of cancer that is depicted the most in the media and it is where our thoughts go to as soon as we hear that our child has got cancer. My first thought was of how much my child loved their hair and how devastated he would be when it started falling out. I admit, the sickness and other nasty side effects took a while to enter my mind.

I can't offer you any iron clad predictions of how you are going to feel. I felt disbelief, then nausea and then anger. It felt unfair that my precious child, one that I had co-created and co-raised, someone I valued more than I would ever value myself, was going to be put through such an ordeal, and the feeling of helplessness was overwhelming. So, I made the decision to cut my long hair off completely, as a gesture of solidarity. My rationale was that I wanted to demonstrate to my child that he wouldn't be on his own when he lost his hair. However, instead of him feeling appreciative and grateful, he took one look at my new hairdo and asked, "what did you do that for?" The reason I am telling you this is so that you can understand that it is okay to want to cut your hair but do it for yourself and not for them. It won't save your child from losing their hair. It's something that you can do to feel like you have more control over the situation and feel less helpless, but nothing more. To a child facing countless rounds of chemotherapy, it's an empty gesture.

Our oncologist told us what to expect from chemotherapy, when it was due to start and what the treatment would look like. We were given a printout that represented different types of drugs and alternating lengths of stays in hospital; round 1 would be a two-night stay, round 2 would be a five-night stay and they would alternate for three months, then he would be scanned. The current size of the tumour would then be compared to images taken at the beginning of the treatment so that a decision could be made on how best to move forwards. Fortunately, we are a blended family, so there are two biological parents and two stepparents. This made alternating nights in hospital easier because there were four of us to share the load. It doesn't matter what kind of family you are, whether you are blended, nuclear or a single parent, it's going to be tough going. But with a schedule, you will be able to work out the logistics of home, work, and hospital. My advice is - don't be scared to ask for help. Help will be available if you ask for it. There were people that offered to babysit my other children, offered a cup of tea and a shoulder to cry on or to drop me off at a train station so that I didn't need to drive. Their kindness absolutely blew me away! As I mentioned before, there are people that run for the hills and people that stay. The latter will offer help because it's all they can do. My advice is to swallow your pride and take it. Take anything they want to throw your way. Let them walk the dog, go grocery shopping for you, babysit your other children or be your taxi driver. Let those who want to help you take the stress of mundane everyday tasks off your shoulders so that you can focus on being there for your child in hospital.

Before your child starts chemotherapy, they may have to have something called a central line fitted. It is known by many different names, but it is a tube that is inserted through general aesthetic into your child's artery, which for us was near his collarbone, and it enables drugs to be administered and blood samples to be taken without the use of needles. To this day, my child still hates having bloods taken and he often says he misses his central line. You will be talked through the procedure and how to care for it during the outpatient appointment after is has been fitted. You will receive lengthy and detailed instructions from a medical professional on how to care for it. It wasn't long before my child was fully competent on how to keep it looped properly on his chest, when to swap over dressings, when to ask for help and so on. It will be a daunting information dump and I honestly didn't retain half of the things they told me before we left. But you will find your feet with this quickly just like I did, plus it comes with a booklet just in case you can't remember everything they

said to you.

The cancer wards are a place that give you an opportunity reframe your mindset to focus on the positive. Where we were, the cancer ward was filled with sliding, frosted glass doors. I was not prepared for seeing children of varying ages walking around in their pj's with a drip trailing behind them, or for hearing their cries in the middle of the night, and I initially saw it as the saddest place on earth. However, over time, I saw it for what it truly was. A place of hope. Children would sit together on sofa's watching a DVD or playing a game of pool. Parents would be chatting in the kitchen whilst they made themselves a cup of tea or microwaving a meal. I realised that it was where children go in the hope of getting better. It is quite easily one of the most hopeful places on earth, where heroes live amongst us dressed in medical gear and armed with reassuring smiles.

A quick note about the incredible human beings in nurse's uniforms, they have seen it all before. They have seen the tears, tantrums, sleep deprivation and starvation, and that's just the parents. They are there with a supportive shoulder, a warm cuddle, and words of comfort. They truly are angels that walk among us, and they do this day in, day out, without ever expecting or asking for any gratitude. I remember that there were NHS strikes going on during our time on the Chemo ward. But these wonderful people chose not to join the strike and remain on the ward where they were needed the most. My advice? Leave your pride at the door on your way in for the first time, and lean on these angels when you need to. Because it won't be a case of 'if', it will be a case of 'when'. It's okay to lose the plot emotionally, it's okay to not want to go through those doors, and it's okay to find it daunting. You're human, you're a parent, and this is your child we are talking about. But these amazing human beings fully understand just how precious your child is and they will do all they can to support you all whilst you are in their charge. My child used to play a game with them that they loved. Because he couldn't remember names very well, he asked each of them their favourite animal. He never forgot one favourite animal; it became almost like a magic mind reading trick that made them laugh and kept him entertained.

These are some of the few ways cancer has helped to change my own mindset. Another way that helped was how I prepared for an overnight stay. I would specifically pick things to eat that I only bought on special occasions, things I was looking forward to eating. I would pack After Eights, a microwaveable Chicken Chow Mein and some Prawn crackers. I would bring some Cadbury's highlights with me, and I would download shows that I was looking forward to watching. Then when my child was sleeping, I would have a midnight feast and binge watch something. Bring things with you that help you feel at home. It felt less alien to me that way. The ward should give you the ability to make hot drinks, microwave food and store things in a fridge, they also had a parent's bathroom so that you could shower if you needed to. I would bring with me reusable cutlery, the 3 in 1 coffee sachets to help save myself from dragging coffee, sugar, and milk with me. Baby wipes are also essential because they are the Swiss army knife of parental life and some nice toiletries from lush to freshen you up with in the mornings. Other things that I found handy to bring with me was a light blocking eye mask for my child because the lights on the ward tend to stay on until its quite late and that can disturb them if they need to sleep before 11pm. I also bought a Bluetooth sleep mask for me because there are alarms on the drip machine that are loud, and nurses aren't always available immediately to turn it off. Chances are, if your drip isn't sounding its alarm, someone else's is. So, it's handy to have a way of drowning that out to get some sleep. Just remember that your child has a call button that will remain in their hand or in their lap whilst they are in bed, so they will press that before they wake you and you will know if you are needed.

In terms of catering to your child's needs, the NHS should take care of their main meals and they came around every day with a menu for them to choose from. However, chemotherapy makes people feel so nauseated that its handy to have a few things to hand for when they are feeling peckish. On top of this, the menu comes around the day before and you have to predict what you think your child will be in the mood to eat, 24 hours in advance, which is tricky. So be prepared to order something with your best educated guess only for them to not want it when it arrives. All too often, I would bring my amazing, well thought out menu to dine upon once my child had fallen asleep, and it ended up with me eating the NHS dinner and him dining out on my stuff! Other times, he would text me his list of foods and drinks to bring in because he wasn't feeling too bad, only for him to feel too rubbish to eat it when I got there. Their appetite and what they feel like eating will fluctuate. I used to end up bringing a big, insulated bag full of things with me to cover all eventualities and leave it there for whoever was taking the overnight shift the next night. One thing I can recommend is something called 'Queasy drops. You can get them online, along with many other boiled sweets specifically aimed at chemotherapy patients. Some people love them, some don't need them. But its handy to have them just in case. I would also like to recommend investing in a sharpie pen and some labels. Everyone on the cancer ward tends to label their food with the patients first name and room number, just to avoid any kind of confusion. Do what works for you and it might take a little trial and error in the beginning, so be patient and see it as a compulsory learning curve.

What your medical team might do, is prescribe some nutrition shakes to ensure that your child is still getting all the vitamins and nutrients they need whilst enduring chemotherapy and its nasty side effects. We were told that they are intended to be a booster meal to add on top of a regular meal, rather than a meal replacement which is usually what we associate nutrition shakes to be for. They may also prescribe other things such as laxatives to ensure that normal bodily functions remain operational. What I am trying to say is, there will be some medication that is easy to get them to take, and others won't be as easy. If you need to hide meds in a drink of squash, do it. If you need to resort to old fashioned bribery, do it. Do what you got to do to get it in them. But don't be afraid to ask for support or advice from those wonderful nurses. It won't be the first time they have had to encourage a child to drink a nasty tasting laxative. Always check with them before you do something if you aren't sure.

Be prepared for this experience to change their tastebuds. They will go off food they adored and might start to like a food they hated. Be prepared for this to be a long-term thing too. My child was a fussy eater before, he has now reached an Olympic level of fussiness thanks to chemo induced nausea. If it's not aesthetically pleasing, he will refuse to eat it.

One thing I did invest in was a mobile wi-fi device. You pay a monthly fee, and the device uses the 4G and 5G cell site signals to produce Wi-Fi that you can log into a use. My child was and still is a dedicated gamer and the NHS wi-fi in the hospital was sketchy at best. When I arrived one day to swap shifts with his dad, I was told that the Tv in the room was broken, and it made an impossible situation even worse. So, I invested in a mobile wi-fi device and even though I signed up to a 2year contract, we called him Dingle Dongle Dave and we took him everywhere we went. Train journeys, hospital stays, car journeys, even when we weren't in hospital, this little device was the hero of the day every single time.

Finally, because chemotherapy wipes out your child's immune system, you will be awarded a small red Medical Alert Card. You will be instructed to look out for a fever of over 38 degrees, being generally unwell, bleeding or bruising and vomiting and diarrhoea. Any of these symptoms whilst at home will win you a first-class ticket to the nearest accident and emergency department. However, because your child's immune system is now non-existent, one flash of this little red card and you will be whisked away from anyone that could contaminate your child with their germs. There is also a list of telephone numbers on the back of the card. If you are ever worried about anything, especially anything that relates to the symptoms on this card, their central line or anything else related to their cancer, they will encourage you to ring them.

Whilst I appreciate that this chapter has been a bit of an information dump, I wanted to share these insights with you as they are based upon my own experience. Yours may vary as cancers and treatments can be as individual as the child being treated. I won't lie, it will be daunting, in ways you didn't know was possible. However, there is a saying in the cancer world that I swear by "you don't know how strong you are until it becomes your only option." I promise you that you are strong enough despite what you tell yourself and I guarantee that you will find a way to move through the phases because even though each phase comes a different storm and despite spending each day trying to keep your head above water, just keep your eye on that beacon of light from the lighthouse. It will remind you that you will adapt, and you will grow stronger. You will not be pulled under the waves.

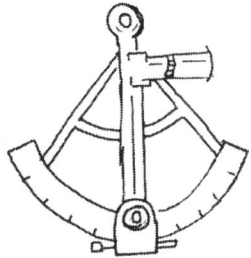

FREDDIE'S STORY

Our 9-year-old son Freddie is the eldest of our 4 children. He is such a happy, kind, and relaxed big brother to his three little brothers, he is an absolute joy to be around. He is our little friend.

Unfortunately, Freddie was diagnosed with a rare childhood cancer in November 2019 at 6 years old. It's called Ewing sarcoma, which was metastatic (in more than one place). It is an aggressive cancer that creates tumours in the bone and soft tissue that can spread to anywhere in the body, very quickly. We had never heard of it (or sarcomas really for that matter) before he was diagnosed. Our world crumbled around us as they told us the news and we stepped into this frightening new world that we would now be living and trying to understand it all.

Stepping in to the ward for the first time seeing children with no hair, tubes everywhere with tall beeping stands at

their side, it hits you like a train...this is really happening.

It started when Freddie complained of chest pain. We assumed it was a pulled muscle from a highly active weekend, but it kept niggling, and we felt it best to get him checked. The GP suggested it was likely to be muscle related and to try Ibuprofen for a week. Funnily enough the pains seemed to settle down a bit, they never disappeared completely and normally came around after something a typical 6-year-old does - a bit of rough and tumble play, making it easy to put down as that triggering it.

A couple of months later, he started to complain of jaw pain, neither our minds nor our GP's mind linked the two together. The jaw pain also came and went initially but it didn't ease off, it got worse, especially at night-time and kept him up every night. The agony worsened so much that after 3 misdiagnoses at the GP surgery (ear infection with antibiotics, TMJ and teething), a lot of pain, blood tests, many sleepless nights where he was inconsolable, antibiotics and above all-precious time, we finally had some progress.

It was from a Locum Dentist we visited after not knowing what else to do one weekend when he was still in pain as the next bit of the GPs advice was still not working. He noticed a slight swelling to his temple, expressed his concern and told us to get to the Oxford A&E to seek a facial specialist at once. We waited for hours but the facial doctor couldn't see us that day, we were anxious but still never suspected anything like what was to come.

We came back the next day and after some scans and having been seen by various doctors, they still didn't have a full diagnosis but simply said, "we don't know what it is yet, but I can't sugar coat this for you, it's not good". That moment and the main diagnosis brings back so much dread, sick, panic, fear. In my head it's obviously bad, but it wouldn't be cancer, it couldn't be.

Freddie has just finished treatment which was a very aggressive chemotherapy regime every two weeks since November, spanning nearly 8 months. He would spend 2 nights a fortnight hooked up to chemo, then the following fortnight would be 5 nights of chemo, meaning in a 28-day period he was in hospital overnight for 7 nights a week. On top of that (especially at the beginning of treatment) he had temperatures between every chemo stint, resulting in him being in for another 2 nights at least on most cycles. We have lost count of how many nights we have spent in hospital.

We are so pleased he has finished chemo, the strain on his little body is heart-breaking to watch. We nurse him better after each cycle and finally get a brief glimpse of our old happy, hyper, crazy Freddie, and then he has to go back into hospital for the next round to be put through it again, on loop for 8 months.

The beginning was so tough, his face was so swollen that his eye was protruding, he was in so much pain with his jaw and a shadow of his old self, but thank goodness the chemo fixed his pains quite quickly from around cycle 2 and we started seeing a glimmer of our boy, he even dealt with the flu on top of all this!

Toward the end of chemo, he then had 6 weeks of radiotherapy everyday (weekends off) with visits taking 3 hours or so out of his day from travelling and treatment.

The last cycle of chemo alongside radiotherapy resulted in him being in hospital for another six nights with mucositis, a temperature and swelling from radiotherapy.

He could barely talk or eat because of the pain and nearly had to have a feeding tube. We managed to fight it off by feeding him (with the tip of a baby spoon, took hours to feed!) of angel delight mixed with double cream and other fatty stuff! He had 5 blood platelet transfusions and 1 blood transfusion in less than 2 weeks as well, which by this time seemed all too normal.

Since the end of treatment, Freddie has been doing really well, with clear scans thank goodness. However, some of the side-effects from the brutal treatment that he endured have shown themselves sadly. Firstly, he now wears glasses as his eyesight has deteriorated, but thankfully he is really pleased about this, and we think he looks awesome! Unfortunately, there are also some signs of cataracts which we were warned about, and it is looking like he will need an operation to remove these at some point in the near future. He also suffers a little bit with scarring to the lining of his lung, which is damage from radiotherapy. Thankfully he doesn't need any intervention, but sometimes he complains of a tight chest which always scares us as parents.

Finally, he has gone through some lengthy tests in regard to hormone levels, and he has been diagnosed with adrenal insufficiency, low thyroid levels, and low growth hormone levels. The first one is managed by medication which he takes three times a day, this has made a huge difference to him as he was feeling very tired, sick and dizzy before this was diagnosed, but it comes with some scary extras.

It is now very important that we always carry an emergency injection with us and give it to him in certain conditions, without this he is at risk of becoming unconscious which as any parent can imagine, is extremely worrying. The low thyroid is another tablet a day. Finally, the growth hormone is still in the pipeline, but it will be a daily injection pen until he is 18 years old or has stopped growing. Of course, this is not going to be easy for Freddie, but low growth hormone doesn't just mean vertical growth, it also has an impact on his heart functions, lungs, and other important areas in his body if he does not receive medication. Therefore, this will be added in the near future.

In any other situation all of this would be such a huge deal, but we will take all of this as long as those scans continue to be clear... I just wish he didn't have to put up with any of this, and that treatment was more advanced, something we will fight for through Freddie's Future, with the aim being to find a cure, so no one has to go through this.

THE EYE OF THE STORM — THE CANCER BUBBLE AND VENTURING OUTSIDE OF IT.

"It is only in sorrow bad weather master's us; in joy we

face the storm and defy it."

Amelia Barr

After a while, you will get used to the rhythm of your new normal. The best way that I can describe it is like the tides of the sea. You will experience surges of activity, where everything seems to happen at once. You will have a scan appointment, medication to collect, a chemotherapy stint on the ward, and if your child gets a temperature that will most likely result in another stay in hospital. Then you will come home and wait for the scan results, which will feel like forever.

It's when the activity comes to a halt, and you're left with just the deafening silence and all the thoughts swirling in your head that you will struggle with the most. I often compare the level of anxiety that this causes to the same way that I felt during my driving test or waiting for the results of my bachelor's degree to arrive.

I found that by rushing from one task to another, it was easier to keep my spiralling thoughts at bay. It was easier to be distracted when I didn't have much time to think. However, I'll be honest, I found returning to the mundane routine of life outside of being a parent with a child battling cancer especially challenging. You want action, you want answers, you want solutions. So, each time things go quiet, it is natural to feel a lack of progress, of stagnancy, even if this isn't actually the case. I don't think I need to tell you that this is a fruitless endeavour that only drains your energy, and I think it's only fair to warn you here that the lulls between bursts of activity often left me feeling like I was in suspended animation where time feels like it passes at a snail's pace. The way life ebbs and flows between activity and inactivity eventually becomes a comfort to you. It gets easier to deal with in time, even though in the beginning doing everyday tasks felt alien to me. I felt that having a child with cancer should be my only focus, by constantly staring at the situation and continuously agonising over it, it would force the matter into some kind of resolution.

However, like I have said before, the housework, grocery shopping and catching up on any outstanding mundane tasks associated with parenthood can offer you a sense of familiarity. These tasks have stayed the same despite cancer's unwelcome arrival in your life as a family. Even though you have no control or influence over how your child's cancer journey began, it is still there. I used to hate doing the housework, laundry and any other tasks that made me sigh and roll my eyes. Now they are the things which remind me that cancer hasn't changed everything. I control when I clean my house, I control what I make for dinner, and I control when I decide to do my laundry. Cancer doesn't control everything in your life. Sometimes you need to remind yourself of that.

Once you get used to life inside your cancer bubble, the time will eventually come where you need to venture outside of it. This can take many forms; it could be anything from grocery shopping, a trip to the pharmacy, or returning to work after having time off to cope with your child's diagnosis.

That being said, venturing outside of the cancer bubble can be daunting and I remember when I left the predictability of my own cancer bubble for the first time, the world didn't feel the same. I found I had less patience for people who drove a little too close behind me and for people who I overheard complaining about how long the check-out queue was in the supermarket. My world was falling apart, and they are complaining about problems that aren't even problems in my world. Cancers unwelcome arrival in your lives does help you to stop agonising over the small stuff. What would have sent me into a stress related frenzy was no longer on my radar as a trigger anymore. I have developed a superhuman level resilience that I use to this day as a result of stepping outside of our cancer bubble.

Once you have ventured outside, the time will eventually come where you will need to make the decision of who you tell and when. There are no rights or wrongs in this decision. You do what you think is best for you and your family. I used the predictability of human nature for gossiping to my advantage. I broke the news to my boss when I said I was taking a few weeks off and asked if she would be so kind as to deliver the news to my team during the next team meeting so that I didn't have to have the same conversation multiple times a day. By the time I had returned to work, those that mattered had already reached out to me and those that didn't know what to say to me were giving me a wide berth as a result.

With time I came to realise that people I encountered either offered a look of pity mixed with relief because this is not happening to them, or they took the scenic route to ignore my gaze entirely. Through these interactions with other people, I found they predictably fell into one of three different interaction related categories. First up are the people who tell you "I don't know what to say to you". They want to offer you words of comfort, but they would prefer to deal with the elephant in the room head on. Second are the people that don't know what to say so they don't talk to you at all. They would prefer not to risk saying something upsetting or triggering, so they avoid you entirely and hope that you can telepathically pick up on them wishing you well from a safe distance. The third and final category are the people that hold the same look of trauma, pain, and resilience that you do. They will meet your gaze and tell you that it isn't fair that that it is crap. One thing I have learned is that trauma of this magnitude is like a magnet, the people who have walked this path before you will come out of hiding and through that moment of connection you will feel seen, your emotions will be validated in a heartbeat, and you will feel safe… treasure these people like stars in your pocket! Sorting interactions into categories also applies to receiving offers of help and support and I have learned that it is like a knee jerk reaction for some. When people say "if there is anything I can do to help" initially it seems genuine, but it can be an unintentionally empty gesture to make themselves feel better. Once you have had the initial conversation breaking the news, they will respond with something along the lines of not knowing what to say and in the same breath offering help should you ever need anything or anyone. Then they disappear off the face of the earth, never to be heard from again. However, there are others who offer help and genuinely mean it. These people will be there with a hot cooked meal, or a lift somewhere, or a cup of tea. No matter how insignificant the task is, they will be willing to drop everything and help, because it's all they can do. This is one of the unspoken truths and unexpected side effects of cancer. It helps you to see who your true, trusted, ride or die friends are. It removes the rose-tinted glasses and the life we lived on auto pilot. I found that although it was painful to lose people that I once considered friends, I was saved the time, energy and emotional pain caused by having to continuously update those that found it difficult to hear. At least this way, I know the ones who ask me for an update genuinely want to know the answer and are ready with a cup of tea (or something stronger) if and when I need it.

These people show that in the middle of the storm where things are sometimes unbearably silent and comfortingly hectic at the same time, there are people who will do whatever they can for you. These people will remind you that you don't need to be a lighthouse for your family all the time, because there are others out there who are ready and willing to be a lighthouse for you if you let them.

NAVIGATING ROUGH SEAS — HOSPITAL STAYS AND SURGICAL PROCEDURES.

"If you start embracing life's storms instead of hiding

away from them, you'll stop fearing them all together; it is

this way one becomes immovable."

Stefanie Scheider.

Okay, I'm not going to lie, this one's is going to be a rough ride. There are a few areas that we need to cover, so I'll start you off easy and we'll work up to the more challenging things. Hospital stays can cover things such as when your child gets a fever whilst they are receiving chemo, they can also cover procedures such as biopsies and even major surgical procedures. Please remember that I am covering these areas with as much of my own perspective and experience as I can. But this does not mean you will experience all of these situations. Because every cancer journey is different.

When your child receives chemotherapy, it wipes out their immune system and they become 'immunocompromised'. It wipes out every injection they have received and the resilience to every bug they have caught. It makes them incredibly vulnerable to catching an infection. So, it's important that they receive medical treatment as soon as possible because the chemotherapy drugs have made sure that they are unable to fight off their infections by themselves. As I have mentioned in previous chapters, you will receive a little red and yellow piece of card, it lists all the things to watch out for during your child's time receiving chemotherapy. One of them is a temperature of 38 degrees or over. This is an indicator of an infection because body temperature rises due to the white blood cells being activated to fight it. When you reach this point and your child's temperature shows as 38 degrees or over, you may be asked to come into hospital so that they can provide medical assistance. Chances are, this won't be an outpatient appointment. You will be placed anywhere where the hospital has space. On one occasion for us, that was the renal ward. Whilst a high temperature can strike at any time, for us it was around 10 days after a round of chemotherapy. Once you have been placed on a ward, your child will stay there until the medical team have the temperature under control. It could be a day; it could be several. There is no set guideline for recovery because it will take as long as it takes, but if you use the same approach as you did for your stays on the chemo wards, it should be more tolerable.

Once chemotherapy starts, bloods will be taken from your child regularly by a community nurse. If anything is showing up as low such as white blood cell count, haemoglobin, or platelets, this can also trigger a visit to hospital as an outpatient for a blood transfusion. This is more likely to be an outpatient appointment, but just beware that just because the round of chemotherapy has finished, that doesn't mean that you are free and clear from unexpected hospital trips in between. My advice would be to get a digital thermometer and keep it somewhere within easy reach at all times. If it needs spare batteries, make sure you stock up.

Moving onto the guaranteed procedure which is the infamous biopsy. We already know this procedure is daunting and ultimately leads to precise diagnosis and treatment. It could be just one biopsy or there could be multiple, and I say this because my child had two biopsies two months apart, both dealt with as outpatient appointments. These will occur before a central line is fitted, so the anaesthetic will be administered via a gas mask. From my experience, gas anaesthetic can make children vomit and feel very nauseous. This poses a problem because the medical team will require your child to eat, drink and go to the toilet before they can be discharged. However, if they are too busy vomiting, it may take them a while to come around to the idea of eating something. On one occasion, we arrived first thing in the morning, and we were there for hours after the sun had set. The other thing to prepare your child for is that the gas anaesthetic has a nasty taste, which is on top of the unnerving experience of having a gas mask placed over their face. If we struggle with gas masks as adults, it must be terrifying for children. However, once the central line goes in, the anaesthetic will be delivered through their line and in our experience, that was a breeze. There was no sickness, no nausea, no dry mouth, and we were in and out from one outpatient procedure within hours. I'm going to let you in on a secret that I didn't know until my child started needing operations - the anaesthetist has a collection of flavoured lip balms that they can rub into part of the gas mask for the anaesthetic which makes the gas taste a little bit more palatable. It became a bit of a game for us where we would sit waiting to be called down the theatre and we would hold discussions about which lip balm he hadn't tried and which he might ask for this time. If your child is small and you think they may be scared of the gas mask going on their face, get their favourite teddy and use a child's asthma inhaler spacer in role playing games at home in the run up. It's not going to remove their fear completely, but it might just help them feel a little bit more prepared for what is to come. Post-surgery, there is nothing wrong with a little old-fashioned bribery to get them to eat and drink. Get their favourite food and drink in advance so that they have something that maximises the chances of them wanted to eat and drink afterwards.

Okay, this next bit explores the things that happen to humans that we push to the very edge of our minds. The things that happen to people that we cannot even try to comprehend. So, if you need to take a break, grab a cup of tea, and sit back down, then please do because this won't be an easy read.

Major surgery covers a vast array of procedures. I can be anything from tumour removal to limb amputation. For us, the two were a package deal. Be aware that the surgery can take hours. Because my child was losing an entire leg, the procedure took four hours. Yours could take less, it could take more, it depends on the procedure. You aren't going to be able to help your child whilst they are in theatre, you aren't going to be any good to them afterwards if you wear out the flooring, pacing back and forth until they return. Try to remember the reason why your child is having the surgery, and that the people you have entrusted your precious child with are experts in their field. My advice is to try and get out of the ward for a while. Even if it is to sit in the hospital café and stare into space whilst you try and make awkward conversations with family members. If the surgery is going to take a significant amount of time, try venturing outside of the hospital for a while. If you are needed to return, the nurses will contact you. Get some space and some distance from the situation. You may think that you won't be able to take your mind off it and whilst that is true to a certain degree, you will find yourself drifting onto thinking about where you are walking to and what you are doing in that moment. That can be all the break that you need sometimes, and with a break comes a refreshed mindset that is ready to take on whatever is coming when you get back to your child's bedside. Once your child returns from recovery and they are now back with you, they may not be completely conscious. They will most likely spend the rest of the day drifting in and out of consciousness. You will want to fuss over them because they are your child, and you want to make it better. Please take this is as confirmation that you are a great parent, that you want to take the pain away and you want to see them smiling again. I'm going to give you a little tough love... you can't do any of these things. Your child and their body will have their own timeline of how long it's going to take to recover. No amount of love and fuss will change that, and they won't be able to share their individual recovery timeline with you either. So, be patient, be there for when they ask you for something and trust that the medical team are there to support you as well as your child. They will do everything they can to get your child well again.

Be prepared for drips and tubes coming out of your child. My child had numerous tubes and dressings, which made it difficult for him to adjust his position in the bed, let alone move around or even get out it. The tubes may include a catheter, which isn't a pleasant experience, no matter how old you are. Just be prepared to help adjust the tubes if your child needs to readjust their position in the bed and bear in mind that this could be in the middle of the night. Another thing is an oxygen mask. My child's oxygen levels would drop every time he fell asleep which would trigger an alarm. So, an oxygen mask was put on him to keep his oxygen levels safe. One thing I was not prepared for was how my child would quickly lose his dignity. Because he was still learning to get out of bed and his catheter had been removed, it meant he had to wear adult nappies. He didn't seem to be bothered by it, but I just wanted to warn you of the overwhelming sense of guilt and helplessness that I felt when I saw him in such a vulnerable state, almost like when he was a baby. Just try to remember that all this, whilst it will be difficult to handle, is to help your child recover from their procedure. By the time you have adjusted, something would have been removed and the demand on your emotions will ease. This recovery period may involve a degree of rehabilitation that involves regular visits from the physiotherapy team. For us, my child had to learn to get out of bed, how to use the toilet and how to walk. After my child had demonstrated that he was recovering from his procedure, the physiotherapy team came every day. Once he had learned how to get out of bed and move around independently, the physiotherapy team came every other day until he demonstrated he could get up and down stairs by himself, then it was only a matter of time before he was discharged.

Nothing will prepare you for seeing your child hooked up to tubes, nothing will prepare you for seeing your child in a level of pain you can't even begin to comprehend. I truly hope that you will never need to use the advice that I have written in this section. Nothing will prepare you for just how useless you will feel. It takes how you felt at your child's diagnosis, their biopsy, their chemotherapy and multiplies it to a level beyond human understanding. You will want to scream, you will want to cry until your lungs burn, you will curse everything and everyone.

Don't shy away from how you feel. Trying to be strong permanently isn't humanly sustainable. Remember, this situation is pushing you to your absolute limit and beyond. So do not feel that you have to bury or hide your emotions. Don't avoid them, do what you can to deal with them. You need to abandon any feelings of being a burden and you must learn to lean on others. Share how you feel with you family, friends, the ones that have said they are there for you and mean it. They will take everything you feel you need to dish out to keep going and they won't mind at all. If you are driving somewhere by yourself and you suddenly get the urge to scream, do it. Do whatever you can but keep moving forwards. Also, try not to make an iron-clad plans during the run up to the procedure or the recovery period. Try to keep them loosely planned if you can. That way you don't have any added stress of trying to remember to call and rearrange something on top of being cooped up in a hospital ward. I know this section has been a harrowing read, but I wanted to keep it real. That's what you are here for. This chapter is written proof that I lived through all of the situations in this chapter, and I still survived. It was a hard slog sometimes, but I am still here, I am still standing, and you will be too. One thing I will say is that as my child is my second born, I can't remember the time he took his first steps. But the second time around, I remember feeling so proud, so grateful and fully present in that moment. It is immortalised in a video clip, but it is a memory I will never take for granted and I shall never forget. Despite everything cancer is doing to keep you in this place of never-ending darkness and struggle, there are incredibly positive things that will happen, like burst of light that will give you the superhuman strength to pick yourself up, stand your ground and tell cancer that it isn't going to take your child without one heck of a fight. No matter how many times the stormy sea of cancer tries to drown you, the lighthouse still stands, and so will you.

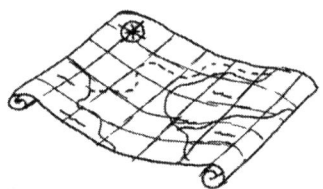

WORDS FROM OUR ONCOLOGIST.

Thankfully, childhood cancer is incredibly rare so the vast majority of the public rarely if ever come across it. As a comparison, we know that 1 in 2 of us will develop cancer at some point in our lives but only 1 in approximately 250 children and young people under the age of 20 develop cancer. As a result, most people view childhood cancer treatment through the lens of relatives or friends who have had treatment for cancer as an adult. Most children and young people tolerate their chemotherapy much better than adults do as children are usually healthier - they don't usually drink alcohol or smoke and are less likely to have other health problems or be overweight. As childhood cancer is so rare, this brings a number of different challenges. Firstly, we only know how to treat different cancers because we can do clinical trials. In most adult cancers, huge trials can be run in only a few hospitals or a single country relatively quickly to have enough patients to clearly tell which of two (or more) treatments is better. In childhood cancer by comparison, clinical trials often have to run for many years and across many countries to allow us to find the best treatment. Whilst working across multiple countries can have positives, it makes the logistics and costs of running the trials much higher.

The second main challenge is to do with developing new treatments. New drugs are very expensive to develop and manufacture so pharmaceutical companies often prioritise areas with large numbers of patients such as breast cancer or type 2 diabetes. There is little financial incentive for pharmaceutical companies to develop and test new treatments in childhood cancer so we often have to use drugs that were developed for adult cancers in the hope they may be effective in children. The majority of childhood cancers are different genetically and biologically to most adult cancers so there is not a lot of crossover between the two. The use of Paediatric Investigation Plans is a legislative approach that ensures pharmaceutical companies have to have a plan for investigating new medicines in children in order to be allowed to use them in adults. Whilst this has helped to widen the number of new drugs studied, it does not change the fundamental problem that these are usually drugs developed for adult cancers being used in children, rather than drugs developed specifically for childhood cancer.

Balancing aggressive treatments with quality of life for my patients is always tricky and is dependent on a number of factors including the type of cancer, the best treatment available and the chances of cure. It is also an individual balance for every patient and family as some children, young people or their parents may put more of a priority on "cure at all costs" whereas others focus more on quality of life. It is absolutely crucial to know that there is no right or wrong answer in the majority of cases, and it needs to be a form of shared decision making between the patient, family and healthcare team.

In some types of childhood cancers which we are very successful at treating, clinical trials are often focused on making treatment less aggressive or toxic without compromising the chances of cure. In some other cancers were cure rates are not as high as we like, we often look at increasing the intensity/aggressiveness of the treatment in an attempt to give a better chance of cure. This is a continual battle between the two extremes but, with better clinical trials and newer treatments, I hope that we will be able to continue to maintain or improve current success rates without dramatically increasing the side-effects.

Coping with the emotional weight of treating children with cancer is tricky and every health care professional dealing with seriously unwell children has different support mechanisms that they can tap in to when needed. I love my job of being able to look after children and young people with cancer which helps. I have a loving and supportive family and church community as well as excellent colleagues. I also enjoy activities outside of work that help me to de-stress such as spending time in nature walking or tending my allotment, reading/listening to music etc.

The two parts of my job that are most memorable come from completely different ends of the emotional spectrum. It is such a delight seeing patients come back to clinic several years after finishing treatment, moving on with their lives and doing all the things you would expect a young person to do. On the flip side, being able to support children and families when all treatments have stopped working is an incredibly special thing to have the privilege to do. Ultimately, we are all working towards the same goal. It can be very frustrating having to "navigate the system" and we share many of those frustrations. We do not always know all the answers but always try our best.

As we learn more about the biology and genetics of childhood cancer, this will open the door ever more to "personalised" medicine. Whilst this is further off in childhood cancer than it is in adults, we continue to learn more every day. This better understanding helps us to design better clinical trials with a higher chance of success.

Using immunotherapy which are treatments that utilise the body's own immune system is a growing field in childhood cancer. CAR-T cells have been completely revolutionary in childhood and adult leukaemia patients and are being studied in a variety of other cancers now with varying degrees of success. We are using a variety of other drugs that act on or in combination with the immune system such as antibodies, cancer vaccines and many others.

We are very lucky to live in a country like the UK where the majority of treatment is available and paid for completely by the NHS. Unfortunately, the majority of children around the world who are diagnosed with cancer every year receive either no or suboptimal treatment due to a lack of resources or understanding or availability of medication. Increasing access to treatment for the majority of children like this could and should be achievable and the International Society of Paediatric Oncology (SIOP) are working with the World Health Organisation (WHO) to try and achieve this.

What stands out to me most about my patients is that in spite of everything that we put them through, they still come back day after day with a smile on their face, and that is incredible. The ability to go on with daily or family life whilst undergoing treatment is genuinely remarkable. Every young person is different and brings their own personality to things.

This is definitely a shared journey between the healthcare team, the patient and their family. It can and should never be all a one-way transfer of information. Having a child with cancer can have a huge impact on the whole family, both during treatment and for a long time afterwards.

THE UNSEEN WAVES — RADIOTHERAPY ...
CUE THE GLOW IN THE DARK JOKES.

"The storm may rage on, it's fury unyielding, but we too,

are relentless — facing it with the same force that keeps us

moving forwards."

Unknown

Okay, so chemotherapy has finished and now instead of being able to catch your breath, you are told you are moving into radiotherapy's neighbourhood. The most overwhelming emotion that I felt at the beginning of this part of our journey was fear of the unknown. I had no idea what to expect or how to forward plan.

We were told that there are two types of radiotherapy: photon and proton. We were temporarily located to Manchester for two months where my son would receive proton beam radiotherapy once a day, 5 days a week, at The Christie Hospital.

The initial reaction was regarding logistics. How on earth were we going to cope as a family when part of the family would be hundreds of miles away? How was my marriage going to survive and what would my relationship with my two other children looked like as a result. Lucky for us, we are a blended family. So, my ex-husband and I organised a rota of days at a time for one of us to be there with our son, and then we would switch. That way, neither of us would be away from our families for very long and it eventually became an event I would look forward to. This was a pleasant yet unexpected side effect because travelling to and from chemotherapy appointments would make me fill up with dread and fear.

This type of treatment differs from chemotherapy, instead of spending days on end in hospital, your child will be treated as an outpatient. You will be provided with a timetable of when the appointments will be each day and they will be given to you weekly. Instead of being constantly confined to a bed with a drip attached, your child will in and out on the same day. The proton beam machines are huge! They are three stories high and involve a big, white igloo looking machine with a bed in the middle of the room. They allow you to have a look at one of them in advance, which is handy for smaller children so that they aren't daunted or scared on the first day of treatment. One thing they may ask to do, is tattoo your child. Don't worry, they aren't going to tattoo a smiley face emoji on their backside or a heart with your name in it on their arm! Whilst it's a very odd request to receive, it's a necessary one because they need to tattoo a few dots around the specific location that the radiotherapy is required so that the laser can lock onto the area where it's needed. Another thing that they will do to prepare your child for their treatment is to get their beanbag ready… yes you read that right… a beanbag. What they do is lie your child down on a beanbag in the position they will be in during their treatment. Then they will suck all the air out of it so that it moulds to your child's specific shape. Then they will lie in their custom beanbag every time they receive their treatment, it just guarantees that they won't move. However, they may be lying in it for a while and there is no way round this because you can't take anything into the treatment room that will potentially help to distract them. My child found the beanbag was comfy and he got into a habit of using his radiotherapy time to have a nap. Then he would be woken up by staff at the end of his treatment and he would have recharged enough to get on with whatever we had planned for the rest of the day.

One side effect of the treatment is dry skin on the area where the laser has been targeting. It looks a lot like the sunburn most of us brits get after a week in Tenerife. You should be prescribed cream to help with this along with instructions of how many times to apply it every day. One of the most vivid memories I have of the time I spent in Manchester with my child was remembering just before bed, when I was dog tired and desperate for sleep that I had forgotten to rub his cream into his treatment site. So, I would be there blinking away the sleep whilst rubbing in the cream for anything up to twenty minutes at a time. To avoid this scenario, I would recommend setting an alarm that reminds you to apply the cream before you get to the same point of parental exhaustion that I did. Another thing to bear in mind is that with anything technological, it is also temperamental. Proton beam therapy is from the United States of America. Its new and we had regular periods of time where our timetable needed to be amended because the machines had broken, and the hospital were waiting for parts to arrive to fix the problem. Because of the tech being American and us being in the United Kingdom, the parts could take a few days to reach us from across the pond. So just bear in mind that no timetable is set in stone.

With long periods away from home, comes a stay in a hotel. We were very lucky with ours. Close to the station, plenty of places to choose to eat from, a shop for groceries and it wasn't too far away from the city centre. The staff were amazing and in the end my child became an honorary receptionist with his own name badge and lanyard. The staff became our friends and even to this day, I still message a few of them. Every time we stay up in Manchester now, we always stay there. It's become a home away from home. The hotel rooms were built like self-catering apartments. We had a combined lounge, kitchen and diner set up with an ensuite master bedroom, a wet room and a second room for my child. The lounge also had a sofa bed so that extra family members could stay there if they were visiting. This gives you comfort in the sense that you aren't under each other's feet all the time, but you also have the choice of staying in and cooking or going out and choosing one of the many local establishments for something to eat. Another thing the hotel had was a transport arrangement with the hospital. There is a bus timetable that runs on weekdays, you would receive a copy of this upon your arrival, and then you should be able to plan what bus to take to get your radiotherapy appointment in time. However, you cannot forward plan for whether the treatment is on time or late. This means that whenever you come out, you could either walk straight onto the bus to get back or you could be waiting a while. If the machines do break down and your timetable changes to a weekend, they will still provide you with alternative transport to the hospital and back. So don't worry, you should have a way to get there and back if you don't have a car, you can't bring it.

I also thought I would point out the obvious … cancer does not have a copy of your calendar and it is possible for treatment to be scheduled on special days. A week into my son's treatment, he turned 13 and the week after that was easter. It's hard to feel normal during a cancer battle and whilst you try your best to inject as much normality into the situation as you can, things like this don't help at all. However, what we did was bring helium balloons up, both sides of my child's blended family travelled up and we spent the day bowling, going to the arcade and walking around the fair outside the Trafford Centre. No, it wasn't the way I expected to spend my child's entrance into his teens. However, it was the first time his dad and I celebrated his birthday together for ten years. This is proof that no matter how hard and how dark things may seem, the silver lining is there if you look hard enough. My advice would be to investigate what is around and plan in advance what you are realistically able to do. See if there is a local supermarket that sells balloons, banners, and cakes and then look at what there is to do in the area local to where you are staying. Remember to work within the energy levels your child has at the time, so that if they have more energy than normal it's a bonus but if they don't, you have already factored that in. The Christie was amazing at still making the day special even though it was a treatment day. I still have photos of my child holding a birthday banner with some of the nurses on his 13th birthday. Work with what you've got and remember that birthdays, Easter, Christmas can all be any day of the year. Celebrate the day in any way you can on the actual day and then plan a huge party for when your child completes their treatment and celebrate with everyone on a grander scale on your home turf.

This approach can also be applied to every day that you are away. Before you travel, work out what there is in the local area to do. We discovered that there is a place that does crazy golf, and it was so much fun that we ended up being regulars. We went shopping, visited Old Trafford and Etihad Stadium, visited the war museum, media city and the cinema, amongst other places. I know things seem dark, disorientating, and daunting, but I really did have the best time in Manchester.

Whilst radiotherapy is a far cry from the Chemotherapy experience, it's still full of its own unique blend of challenges. It's still going to test your resolve, your resilience, your motivation, and how secure your hold is on a positive mindset, it's just going to test you in a different way. Prepare yourselves for what you might see when you are in the waiting room. Children may appear that remind you that this is their last shot of staying alive. Hold onto the fact that this is where people use technology to challenge what feels like the impossible. This is where technology steps in and does its best to tell cancer it's time to leave. This is a place where people move heaven and earth to keep families together and to save as many lives as they can.

The hotel we stayed at truly made a difference to our experience. We made friends with other families that were in the same position as ourselves. We shared pizza nights in each other's hotel rooms and the staff became like our extended family. They did all they could to make sure we felt as at home as possible. They let you bring home comforts with you, and whilst I don't mean your favourite armchair, I mean things like the x-box, a laptop, some new Lego sets, anything that you think might make your child's stay less stressful and more like home, just ask the staff before you get there, and they will do their best to help you. There was always something to do and whilst I can't remember everything that we got up to in that two-month period, I look back now and remember the constant laughter, the random people coming up to my child and telling him that he's a hero, or that they would look forward to seeing him in the Paralympics, and the café staff that recognised us and welcomed us to our favourite seat. One major thing you must remember, is that you cannot spend your entire time during radiotherapy wondering whether this will be the treatment that either cures or fails to cure your child. Our stay in Manchester for radiotherapy taught me that Cancer may win in the end, it may not, but it cannot touch the positive memories that I created with my child whilst we were there. I hope you receive a similar experience to ours. This is a sliver of proof that in the midst of a storm made of uncertainty, our lighthouse showed us that there were always moments of light when we needed them the most and helped us feel more able to endure the darker times.

THE LIFEBOAT – SIBLINGS: THE FORGOTTEN SUPERHEROES.

"The storm rages, but I remain a quiet force within it,

unseen yet grounded in the moment."

Unknown

Just because you've broken the news to your child that they have cancer doesn't mean that you are now free from having that conversation again. If you have more than one child, this means you are faced with having it again. I have two other children aged 8 and 16, and this meant that I would have to have this conversation twice more but in opposing ways.

Just like you factored in the personality, temperament and cognitive capabilities of your child who has cancer, this must also come into play when you assess the best way and the best time to talk to your other children about it.

My oldest is two years older than my child with cancer, so she was a third of her way into her teens when her younger brother was diagnosed. Whilst we did our best to shield them all from the situation until we had more facts. children are far more perceptive and observant than we give them credit for. My oldest knew what the situation was way before we told her. Not only that but she correctly predicted every next step before we as parents had even been told. What I'm trying to say is that sometimes, despite our best efforts to protect our children, they are miniature detectives who are determined to solve the of mystery of why things have changed at home, regardless of how many times you try to pacify them until you are in the right mindset, have all the facts at hand to be able to talk about it. Being eight years apart and very different individuals, my other two children were polar opposites in how they dealt with it. My youngest child immediately demonstrated that he knew he needed to step back and demand less because my focus was elsewhere. He embraced being a sibling of a child to cancer and he still shows pride in it to this day. It has become a badge of honour for him, and he refer to his brother as his hero. Whilst conversations with him on the subject are few and far between, its these behaviours that reassure me he is dealing with it on his terms and in his own way. However, I do need to warn you, we know that younger children such as mine tend to use logic and the limited information children have about a situation when they are trying to understand something. In relation to Cancer, all my youngest knew was that cancer kills people, so naturally his assumption was that his brother was going to die. This is where a charity called Molly Ollys Wishes came to my rescue. They do a spectacular range of books that help both the child with cancer and their siblings to understand what's going on in a sensitive, respectful and child friendly way. They also offer an Olly the Brave teddy who is a lion that comes with his own central line fitted and a removable mane. I cannot recommend them highly enough and I will put their details in the charities and seeking help chapter further along in the book.

For my oldest, I took a different approach. Long before her brother was diagnosed with cancer, we had developed a weekly tradition of going for a coffee on a Sunday morning. No matter what was going on, no matter how chaotic things were or how many hospital visits we had, I made sure we had our Sunday morning coffee time. This is where we would take a beat and exist outside of the cancer world if we needed to. But it also doubled up as a space where were gave ourselves permission to talk about what was going on if either of us had something on our mind. I had a rule that whatever was said in the coffee shop stayed in the coffee shop and she used this weekly tradition as a place where she could get things off her chest. Even now, we still do Sunday coffee mornings and a mooch around the shops. It's our time and it has become the backbone of our relationship which has only strengthened through this journey. When I look back to our most recent holiday abroad all you can hear in the videos is my daughter and I laughing and putting on silly accents. So, whilst cancer may try to rip my whole world to shreds, it has made my relationship with my daughter stronger. I am proof that it's not always raining in cancer land… sometimes there are rainbows if you know to look for them.

Whether your other children are chatterboxes that have endless amounts of questions, or they don't talk at all, just know that they are processing it in their own way. Either way, how they feel will either come out during conversations or through their behaviour. Brace yourself for them potentially feeling overlooked because you are anxious, stressed, or exhausted. The unseen battle is that cancer will change their identity too because it's going to change from being a person in their own right to the sibling of a child with cancer and this label is very sticky, it isn't shaken off easily. Furthermore, if they achieve anything during their sibling's cancer battle, the reality is that they aren't going to be recognised in the same way as they may have been before this. I know that this isn't an exclusive list, these are a few things that cropped up during our battle and my hope is that whilst some of these feelings aren't going to be avoidable, by being aware of them in advance, you can be more self-aware of what is going on and how you can support them. Try not to attempt to remove the feeling altogether because it's just not realistic or sustainable and try to accept the fact that all you can do is damage limitation.

Just like their sibling, they will have their own timeline and method of processing the fact that cancer has changed the landscape of the family forever. No amount of influence or strategic planning on your part will force them onto the path that you feel is the best way to process what is going on. For some children they will deal with it through action and hitting the situation head on, some will deal with it through talking, and others will just stay in their lane because that's all they can do. One thing that does have a possibility of making an appearance is the same question you keep asking yourself: "why them? Why not me instead?" They have the same potential to be lost in a sea of despair, disorientation, and guilt, and it's up to you to steer them back to shore.

I have always used the analogy of being a lighthouse, both personally and professionally, and this could not be any truer in this situation. It is not your job to force them back to shore, it is your job to keep that light shining, being that fixed point of reference for them, guiding them back to love, reassurance, and safety. I'm not saying that will be an easy task, but I do want to make sure that you give yourself permission to just 'be'. To be there, be consistent and be the light for your children who feel just as lost and helpless as you do. You do not need to force things, just let them know that you are all in the same boat together, that you don't know where things are going to lead you, but if you keep your eye on the lighthouse, you will always know where home is and that is what truly matters in all of this.

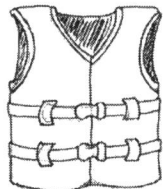

MENTAL HEALTH ADVICE FROM A COUNSELLOR.

You might think, in these pages, that you are reading about a remarkable boy and his brave and extraordinary mother. You might look at those stories of brave children with cancer, and other life shortening illnesses and disabilities, and admire their cheerfulness, their resilience, and the way their families and communities gather around – raising funds for trips abroad; ticking off experiences on their bucket lists; meeting footballers and celebrities.

When I look at these children and their families, however, I see ordinary people wishing beyond wishing that they weren't extraordinary or different; that they were, in fact, as ordinary as anything. Families whose lives didn't revolve around tests, and hospital visits, and breathing a sigh of relief every time they hear that the cancer hasn't spread. Or gathering up hope and courage again when they hear bad news.

My job, as a counsellor and psychotherapist, has been focussed on talking with people about their pain – about the circumstances they find themselves in. Mostly these contexts and situations are not of their making. Cancer, like many other illnesses and disorders that can affect us all – including sometimes children – can seem like a lottery ticket from hell. Why does this child contract it? Why does that child stay healthy? There will be reasons, of course, in the physiology and genetics and sometimes the ways these combine in a particular set of environmental circumstances, but to those affected it can seem like a bolt from the blue.

Why me? Why us? The questions can never really be answered.

Meanwhile the child and parents and siblings – and the wider social

and relational networks around them – have a new reality to face; one they never imagined. One that the rest of us can only imagine. I'm a therapist - but I'm also a dad and a grandpa – and when I listen to the stories of people like Jacob and Claire, I imagine what it must be like for them. It's hard because my own relationships get in the way. I imagine what it would be like if one of my granddaughters was in Jacob's shoes.

I imagine what it would be like to be in Claire's shoes – as Jacob's mother. I imagine, but also try – because that's the job I've chosen to do – to understand the depth of the pain they must experience, and what it takes from them to be all the things that others see in them – the courage, the cheerfulness, the hope.

I don't want to take away these positive things. Each moment in life is a moment in which we can experience joy. Millions of people, who aren't suffering from illness or loss, can nevertheless find themselves drifting through life, not noticing what it's like to be alive!

Which can be amazing. And can also be crap.

So false positivity is not a great thing – it obscures what people are really feeling, and that's never a great thing – even when sickness and loss are not (for them, for the time being) the main story. It's also true that facing grief every day is unmeasurably hard and can grind down and destroy people. This can be true for the person who is ill and might be dying, and the people around them who care for and love them. Living with despair is also not a great thing. Not all the time. It's going to be there sometimes – it is for all of us in some ways in this strange and broken world – but where loss is closer than it seems it should be, despair is never far away.

Claire has described it as a monster clinging to her back; a shadow creature that is always there, but that, sometimes, she has to negotiate with.

Just give me some time to enjoy this, she might ask. Just let me sleep. Laugh. Work. Love. Enjoy this bit of today. Just give me a rest so I can carry you again tomorrow…

Because, living with grief for someone who is still alive but someday may not be, is nothing less than exhausting. The pain is bad enough, but the grinding tiredness can be worse. Which is why the acceptance of this awful existential reality needs a big dose of compassion and self-compassion, as well as seeing the good, the bad and the drearily ordinary (which is often the biggest relief), all together in the experiential 'now'.

Now is all there is. Claire and I talked about that a lot. What was in the past – Jacob's diagnosis, all the initial disbelief and distress, all the shocking emergence of chaos and subsequent reaching out for hope and miracles, are in the past. What is in the future is… well, uncertain in many ways. Though the ultimate end of the story might be known that chapter is not yet written as we sit in a room together talking. Today, you are dealing with getting your daughter from here to there, and you are sorting out some tedious but necessary problem at work. Today you are having a difficult conversation with someone about a family issue, buying Jacob another bottle of his favourite Eau de Cologne, and telling him off because he's been a bit of a cheeky monkey. Today, you are making up Star Wars stories as metaphors for your family's realignment and readjustment. Today you are making people laugh – at themselves, at you, at the situation and the fucking awful reality that someone is dying sometime in the future and shouldn't be.

The future, though, is not here yet, and all that is projection - for now. There are loads more moments of joy and pain and ordinariness to get through and experience before then.

Claire asked me to write something about what a parent or carer can do to support themselves through the kind of experience that she is going through with her son Jacob's illness. It's really not an easy question to answer. Each person – each family – is different and each individual will have their own ways of getting through this life that includes, in the very warp and weft of its fabric, death, loss and illness.

However, I guess, I would say that the first thing to do might be to recognise the <u>need</u> to support yourself. You will be the main person (or persons) supporting your child through what is a frightening, confusing and possibly devastating facing of the reality of their life ending. We all have to face death, of course, but when a child dies – or faces death – it feels unnatural, to them as much as to us. A glitch in the fabric of what the world should be, even if we know, rationally, that it's just as ordinary as anything less in life.

You will feel extreme anxiety, anger, pain, stress, and guilt, and you may work hard to overcome these emotions and feelings; to hide them from others, to override them with positivity and stubborn invulnerable bravery. This can come at a dreadful cost. However, maybe what you need - and maybe what your child needs - is for you to be in touch with your vulnerability. To be honest with yourself about what this thing feels like and to have a place, a space, and a person (or more than one), where and with whom you can empty out yourself and to admit to yourself that you are not in control of everything, and nor should anyone expect you to be.

And then we come to love. The one thing we can be good at – in this now, with this sick and possibly dying young person who we are supposed to protect and care for - who we have always protected and cared for - is LOVE. We can be good at loving them – and the other people in our lives.

Love is ordinary, actually. It's not remarkable. It's just what we are all capable of and open to. Though sometimes when the practicalities of life and the difficult and tragic circumstances it brings seem to overwhelm and consume us, we can forget this simple, human truth. When we love each other – in the here and now, not in the twisted past, or the imagined future – it might be possible to support and care for ourselves through these awful and difficult times. And when things end, when people die, love is also what holds them in our hearts. They become ripples on a pond, waves on the ocean, racing out as memories – touching everyone with love we held for them.

Sometimes, this is very hard to do; to hold love and face it when everything feels so painful. But humans can do this. It is the best of us. Sometimes we might need some compassionate help and a listening ear to help us with this task. Sometimes we will struggle and break down and feel as if the world as we know is ending. And it is, of course, but that's all part of the new now, and it is OK (though it may not feel OK for a long time).

In short (and this piece has been longer than I imagined!), there is no easy answer to the question of what we can do to support ourselves in circumstances where a child - or a loved one - is dying. What may be true, however, is that the child or loved one might need us to find our own answer to this question; and that this might mean being humble about our own certainties and talking to someone who might have a little wisdom to offer.

In the end, the whole phenomenon of death and dying is a mystery. All we can do is live with the things we know, and the love we hold for the people in our lives. Doing the ordinary things, and keeping the window of our imagination open, but just enough so that we can bear it.

Not agonising about the past, not fearing the future (which will come in its own time and form), but living in the here and now, with all the messiness, grief, laughter, and tears that might come.

Bring it all on, I guess I might say, it's all part of how we love each other....

TRYING NOT TO CAPCIZE – CAREGIVER BURNOUT: FILLING THE CUPS OF OTHERS WHEN YOURS IS EMPTY.

"Great sea captains are made in rough waters and deep

seas."

Kathryn Kuhlman

Right from the start, you will feel like you have been magically transported onto a hamster wheel and you have no idea how to get off. Whilst I am also writing a chapter on mental health, caregiver burnout is its own beast, so I felt that it deserved its own space. Burnout is not a sign that you aren't strong enough to cope with everything that's going on, it's a sign that you have been too strong for too long.

Stepping off the hamster wheel is a lot easier said than done. You have the weight of the world on your shoulders. You will be carrying a lot of blame – "should I have done something sooner?", a lot of anger – "why my child?" and the guilt over not having enough time for your partner or your other children.

On top of this, you will be dealing with a whirlwind of emotions whilst you are away from home. The same four hospital walls, the same walk to the hospital cafeteria, the same tv channels and the same battle with getting enough sleep. If any of you have seen the tv programmes about being in the SAS or similar military organisations, you will know that sleep deprivation is used as an interrogation technique. For those of you that find this as new information… your welcome. The reason for this is because going without enough sleep is enough to push someone to the brink of insanity. But the reality of your situation is that you will probably be struggling to sleep anyway. Once treatment starts, there will be beeping machines, an overwhelming level of anxiety and the worry of your child needing you whilst you are sleeping added to the mix. You will also be managing your child's medication, keeping them stocked, asking for prescriptions, and convincing your child to actually take them. These are the perfect conditions for burnout.

The way I dealt with cabin fever in hospital was to make a list of films that I have always wanted to watch with my child, we made a film bucket list and every time we were on the ward together, we'd strike a few off. This has now become an integral part of our family life because my child always has a film in mind ready for the weekend. Some of the best traditions that we have now were formed during our time in hospital because we were looking for ways to manage the demands on our mental, emotional, and physical health. I remember that I was finishing my bachelor's degree at the time my child was diagnosed. At that point, I had been doing five part-time years at university and I had one year left. I asked him in the beginning if he wanted me to defer for a year so I could focus on his treatment. I will never forget the look he gave me, like I had just lost my mind. Then he shook his head and said "you've come this far mum. There is no way you're quitting now!" Looking back, I am grateful for having it as a distraction. I would be sitting on the pull-down bed next to him with my laptop, textbooks, highlighters, and a notepad. I would study when he was sleeping, and it provided me with a much-needed break. My degree was something that I could control, something that existed outside of the cancer world, and I threw myself into it wholeheartedly.

However, this meant that I was dancing with burnout a lot. It wasn't that I felt things would fall apart if I stopped, it was that I worried if I stopped moving I would start thinking about what might be and I didn't want the fear of losing my child to cancer to swallow me whole. People say that they are 'afraid' of things all the time. But this is the sheer, undiluted terror of losing your child that can leave you awake in the middle of the night, drenched in a cold sweat and hyperventilating. My coping mechanism was to pack my day to the brim with so many things to do that I didn't have time to think. The consequence of this was that I was constantly burning myself out in an attempt to keep away those very specific demons that lurk in the furthest, darkest corners of my mind. From my own experience, once you become too afraid to stop, it becomes a very difficult habit to break and the reality of the situation is that sometimes you will need to make a choice between burning yourself out and sitting with your thoughts. Yes, if you stop, dark thoughts may make an unwelcome appearance but if you keep going you become too exhausted to fight them anyway. At least choosing to sit with those thoughts means that you are doing it on your terms. The best piece of advice that I am only just learning how to do is to get used to sitting with the elephant in the room. To get comfortable with its company and learn to live with it instead of spending all your time fighting with it. Its counterintuitive because we are taught to avoid the things that hurt. I hate to be the one to break it to you, but you can't outrun this, and you can't avoid it forever. So, the sooner you learn to sit beside it without fighting it, the more peace you will find.

I have learned to recognise that I am burning myself out through what I call 'task stacking.' It's the phrase I use when family life creates tasks that all stack up on each other. Once I get to a point where I can't remember all of the tasks, it's time to tap out. Depending on the number of tasks and the time of the day, the amount of time I take for tapping out can vary. Sometimes it's taking the dog on a quick walk round the block, other times it's sitting in the garden with a cup of tea and a book, or even putting a do not disturb sign on the bathroom door whilst I have a much-needed soak. The way I see it, even mobile phones need recharging and there are multiple things that are currently draining your battery at a significant rate. So, learn to be okay with stopping.

I'm not going to sugar coat it, learning this isn't going to be easy because you've spent your whole life as a parent constantly giving someone else everything you have. It's now ingrained in your behaviour and perspectives, and you may struggle to avoid burn out because you have been telling yourself that if you stop, everything is going to fall apart. Please believe me when I say that this isn't true. Because the reality is that constantly pushing yourself beyond your limits isn't strength, it's a coping mechanism that just empties your cup faster. Try to keep in mind that once your cup is empty, you'll have nothing left and you won't be able to help anyone and that is when things will fall apart! The most important message in this chapter is that you need to give yourself permission to stop without feeling guilty or beating yourself up over it. There is a lot happening right now and the only person expecting you to keep it together all of the time is you. If it was happening to someone else, you would show them compassion, so make sure you show the same courtesy to yourself without beating yourself up for it. Even though lighthouses are strong and unyielding no matter the weather, even they need some maintenance because if the light burns out, there will be nothing to guide those who rely on it back to shore.

LOST AT SEA — MANAGING MENTAL HEALTH: UNTANGLING A BALL OF STRING.

"When the storm rips you to pieces, you get to decide how

to put yourself back together again."

Bryant H. McGill

Just like it is for any other situation, your mindset can either mean you win, or you lose. Whilst it isn't as cut and dried as that in the cancer world, the sentiment behind it is the same but it's a much larger, scarier prospect. You are being tested in ways that people who are fortunate enough to not be a part of this world cannot possibly fathom. This isn't a get out of jail free card or an excuse to take your frustrations out on other people, it's a constant choice first thing in the morning to have a positive mindset, to be the best version of yourself each and every day. The reality is that from the moment you heard the word cancer, you have been learning to live with uncertainty. You are learning to live with the emotional agony of watching your child fight for their life. Even then, when you are doing your best and you feel like you have a handle on your moods and perspectives, you always carry the situation around on your back. You are doing your best to keep your family going, to keep your head above water and at the most random moments, your thoughts will wander off to the restricted section in furthest corner of your mind where all your dark thoughts are lurking. Please remember that none of these thoughts are based on facts, only fear, and whilst it's okay to be scared, don't set up camp in that neighbourhood. I tend to shush those thoughts aloud and tell them that I am busy. That seems to be enough for me to regain control of the situation before I begin to nosedive. Because the thing with nosedives is that you can't guarantee that you will be able to pull yourself out of it, and if you can't? What good are you going to be to your family?

In the book "The Courage to be Disliked," by Ichiro Kishimi and Fumitake Koga, the philosopher touches upon a concept with the student. He introduces the perspective that whilst something may not be your fault, it remains your responsibility to deal with it. So, whilst it isn't your fault that your child is battling cancer, it is your responsibility to keep your mental health in peak condition so that you can help them to fight it as best they can. Mental health isn't an option on your 'to-do' list that you can pick up and drop at your convenience. It should always and is always your MVP, regardless of what you're facing.

At the beginning, I was given a piece of advice. I was told to get used to not seeing my other children and to accept the possibility that this might break my marriage. Whilst I am happy to report that this was not the case for my husband and my other children, this is sadly a reality for some families enduring this nightmare. If you are not home because you are supporting your child in their cancer battle, it is going to be hard to keep your marriage on solid footing and maintain a positive relationship with your other children. But it's not impossible. I would recommend that you look into getting counselling as soon as you can. I know you are struggling to think of where in your life you are going to find time to do it, but I promise you that you are going to need someone to vent to that isn't in the trenches themselves. You will need someone impartial that can offer you support without you feeling like you are burdening someone who already has an impossible weight to carry. I invested in counselling as soon as my son was diagnosed, and it is an investment in protecting my mental health that I will always be grateful for. My mental health is my suit of armour and without it, I wouldn't be able to take on half of the blows that cancer has dealt me. I would also get in touch with the school your children go to and ask if they have counselling or pastoral support that they can offer. This is in addition to keeping the school it ensures that staff can be ready to support them if needed, but anything extra that they can do is an added bonus. However, even though you are protecting your mental health by talking to a professional, that doesn't mean you shouldn't also be talking to your partner. You need to share what is going on in your head with them because they need to have your back in this fight, and you need to have theirs and you can't do that unless you talk. You need to share all the dark, gritty stuff because it's only then that you can fight in this battle against cancer together. You won't be able to do that if you are on different pages mentally and emotionally. The way my husband and I did it was through our mutual love of television and films. If there was a program on that we liked to watch but one of us was at home and the other in hospital, we would watch it at the same time whilst on a video call and we would talk just like we were on the sofa together. Even if we weren't watching anything we would video call, we would always say goodnight to each other. It seems like a silly thing to do but it's the little things that eventually act as the glue that holds you together as a couple. Cancer affects areas other than just our relationships with our loved ones. Whilst I hope you have a supportive employer; this is sadly not the case for everyone. Some will say you can take whatever time off you need and all they ask is to be kept updated and others will outline the expectations for you to uphold your responsibilities. This is not a nice situation to be in and it can take you to the brink of breaking point if you have to worry about keeping your job on top of everything else. My advice is to look into joining a union at the very beginning so that you are covered from the start and to look into charities that can help alleviate some of the financial burdens on you that come with having a child fighting cancer. I have put a list of a few charities that can potentially offer financial support. Finally, please try to remember that if you do get to a point where you are struggling or you think someone in your family is struggling, please seek the help and support of your doctor. I was fortunate enough to receive counselling through my employer. But I was also offered counselling and mental health support through my doctors' surgery. The bottom line is that suffering in silence isn't brave, it's dangerous. You can't' help anyone if you aren't helping yourself and that's why you are told on a plane before take-off to put your mask on before you do it for others. The one thing I did when my child was diagnosed was get the Avengers symbol tattooed on my right wrist. This was to remind me that there is no shame in asking for help and that if you do, help will come. The thing I have learned from my toxic relationship with cancer is that it helps to put everything into perspective, and you'll find you won't agonise over the small stuff as much. I say that now but if cancer isn't enough to cure my road rage, I am pretty sure that will be with me forever! I tend to work with facts, if it doesn't come from the mouth of our oncologist, I tend to either treat it with a pinch of salt or dismiss it completely and I only deal with the present. I have a rule that if a situation isn't kicking my door down like an FBI agent on a drugs raid, I can return to it when it is. There are some days where I can tackle the whole day with very little effort and there are others where I have to take it an hour at a time. It waxes and wanes, but you will get used to the rhythm and you will find your own way to keep your suit of armour in peak condition, as long as you understand that it will take constant dedication. There will always be another storm on the horizon, ready to test you in a different way. But if you keep your eye on your lighthouse, you won't feel the need to spend all your time bracing yourself for it to hit you.

PAIN INTO PURPOSE: PARENTS WITH THE HEARTS OF LIONS.

Nicole

A lot of people ask me how Freddie is doing now when they hear his story. Of course, I answer that he is doing well minus the side-effects. But I think what people really mean is what is his future like? what is his prognosis? Sometimes people do ask me that, but they apologise for asking. I think people all know that having a childhood cancer is never going to be good… but they don't like asking and they don't understand what brutal treatment we have been through. They don't seem aware that it wasn't just something like a bone that broke that is now okay, there is so much more to it than that when looking to the future when you have been through something like this. I think it is important to talk about prognosis, because part of the problem of lack of research and brutal treatments is that sadly prognosis is poor for a lot of childhood cancers. If there was more research, kinder treatments, and a lot more funding available for childhood cancers it wouldn't be such a taboo subject, and it wouldn't be so hard for parents to talk about.

It is also extremely hard to decide what you do and don't tell your child and how you talk to them about it, especially as specialists talk in front of them. As they grow older, of course things change, and they ask more questions and understand more too.

Despite talking about poor prognosis, I don't think you can live your life assuming the worst. When it comes to science, I have really learnt that nothing is definite, nothing is set in stone... You could be that 2% that statistics don't talk about that actually turn out to be okay in the end. Also, statistics change so much and a lot of the time we just don't have the data for them to be accurate. So, if I was giving myself advice - I'd say always think positively and think of your child as their own journey, not a statistic as you just don't know what the future will throw at you, every story is different. I definitely remember reading statistics when he was first diagnosed and focusing on that so much as they are terrifying statistics for metastatic Ewing sarcoma. Yet here we are nearly 5 years later. Something I will never take for granted. I would also join any Facebook groups or support groups that have fellow parents in… Whether that's a general childhood cancer group, or your specific cancer group. By reading stories of hope and speaking to others it really helped me to stay positive and focused. But it also kept me balanced as I saw lots of different stories about lots of different scenarios. It also gave me a place to feel anonymous and ask questions to those who understood. I felt powerless when a whole team of doctors took over the care of my child and I couldn't make it better for him anymore. I felt like I couldn't just kneel down and put a plaster on his cut and give him a cuddle and make everything better… It was so much more than this, so much more than I was able to give. I couldn't protect him from this monster that was making him so poorly. That really hurt and I felt so helpless… you just put their life in someone else's hands and even though you know it is the right thing to do…. It just doesn't feel natural as a parent.

I took the power back by starting Freddie's future through the bone cancer research trust… A charity that fights for better, kinder treatments for bone cancer - exactly what I hope for having been through all this alongside Freddie. By doing that, I feel like I am making a difference and doing something positive. We are a tiny charity with a big thing to fight, and fighting for improvement gives me a feeling of getting some power back.

Mark

Stepping into the role of stepdad to a young child wasn't ever something I remember being daunted by because his time was shared between my wife and his biological dad. We had time for ourselves as a couple and time as a family, so it wasn't as intense as I know the situation could've been. Over the years, our bond has grown through a mutual love of football, a similar sense of humour and the countless toys I have had to consult instructions over to piece together for birthdays and Christmases.

When he was first diagnosed, I felt shock, disbelief and I remember my first thought being if that meant he was going to die. I knew that meant we had a long process of hospital appointments and that I would not be able to attend most of them because we had our own child who had just turned six that I would have to stay at home and look after because we had no family locally to help with babysitting. I knew that this meant I wouldn't be able to attend cancer related appointments as much as my wife or her ex-husband and I would be receiving information from these appointments second hand, sometimes even third hand. This is frustrating but I tried to remind myself that this hadn't changed my role as stepdad. There are moments throughout the cancer journey that you just cannot prepare yourself for, no matter how hard you try. After all, it's not a situation you ever imagined you would be in, so you can't ever fully prepare yourself for it. It will make you feel helpless and there will be times that it makes you feel like you can't breathe, but you have to keep moving forwards; you don't have a choice. When he was having a bad day due to treatment or recovery, I would do whatever any other parent would do. I offered reassurance, advice, support or whatever else he needed at the time. If he needed me to sit with him, I would. If he needed me to distract him with a joke or by putting a film on tv, I would. That part of my role hasn't changed, and I don't think it does regardless of whether you are a biological parent or a stepparent. This also applies to my wife too; I will do whatever I can to offer her what she needs. However, it usually comes when she is spiralling on 'what if's', and I step in by offering the support in the form of reminding her of the latest scan results. I find that focusing on facts and quoting the oncologists words from the latest appointment is a supportive way to pull her out of it. The thing is, life before my step-son was diagnosed with Cancer does not compare to life afterwards. Before, he was healthy and my life revolved around worrying about materialistic things such as the car, my job, money, and things like that. Whilst my role as his stepdad hasn't changed in its functionality, cancer does change your perspective because you can only focus on the short-term. It tends to take off the rose-tinted glasses and help you not to take the little things for granted. What this journey has taught me is that I am more resilient than I thought I was, and that cancer has helped me to become far more resilient than I was when this journey began. My wife tells me that my support is invaluable and without me holding the fort at home and giving our own child a sense of normality, she would not have been able to attend half of her older son's cancer appointments. She also says that she would have fallen apart right at the start of the journey and that she draws her own strength from me being one of the only constants in her life.

My advice for other stepparents is that your role doesn't change. There are other things that you can bring to the table rather than just going to appointments. Your role is more aligned with offering pastoral support for siblings and the rest of the family. There are more people being affected by this journey than just the child who is battling cancer. By supporting siblings and maintaining a sense of normality at home, you are helping to take some of the weight off your partners shoulders so that they can focus their support where it is needed the most. If you have any questions for oncology appointments but you can't be there in person, write them down and ask your partner to take them along. My wife used to record the appointment on her phone in

the beginning and bring it back for me to listen to so it still felt like I was receiving information first-hand. If you miss your stepchild because they are in hospital, try to facetime as much as you realistically can so that you can maintain that relationship with them. The most important is communication; if you are getting frustrated by being stuck on childcare duty with another child, or if you are feeling like you are being left out of the loop, say so. Honest and clear communication with your partner is key here. But remember to do it from a calm place where your intention is to be heard and to work with them to find a mutually beneficial resolution. If you approach a situation with a desire to have a rant, it isn't going to resolve anything. In fact, it will probably only make things worse and make it harder to find a solution further on down the line when neither of you are able to ignore it. Choose your moment wisely and make sure it isn't after your partner has had a long stint in hospital with your stepchild when they are overtired, absolutely exhausted, and probably on the edge of losing it already. Just remember, that even though you may feel like everything around you is changing, it doesn't change your role as the main source of support for your immediate and extended family. Don't feel like your role isn't as important just because you are a stepparent and not a biological parent.

Andrew

When my son was diagnosed, all I remember is feeling shocked. I don't remember much else. Other than that, I remember spending my time trying to focus on things that I could control. I would concentrate on making sure that medication was stocked and administered on time because that was all I felt I had control of. During my son's treatment, I would do my best to find experiences for him. I wanted to make sure that he experienced as much of the world and what it has to offer as I possibly could. It has bought us so much closer together as father and son and I am grateful for all the cancer charities that have supported us by arranging all the wonderful things we have been fortunate enough to experience. It is through these things that I have made friends that will stay with me long after this battle is over. The hardest part I found was feeling like I was in a goldfish bowl. Looking out of hospital windows at the world, watching everyone else but me and my son going about their day as normal and the claustrophobic feeling of cabin fever creeping in.

My advice to other parents is to be patient. It's a longer journey than you realise and whilst you will want to do everything you can right from the start, by doing that you will be using all your energy up in the beginning and you won't have enough left for the rest of the journey. I would also say that it is important to trust the medicine and to be open and honest with the doctors. They are the experts, so if you need advice, don't be afraid to ask.

Fee

"I'm so sorry, but it's childhood cancer."

Those handful of words shatter your world, bringing an avalanche of heartbreak, chaos, pain, and sheer devastation. It can't be my child; it has to be a mistake. They say it's rare, but in this moment, it feels all too real.

And yet, here you are, thrust into a new reality where hospital stays become the norm and the whirlwind of appointments transforms your daily life. Suddenly, you're on a first-name basis with nurses and doctors, navigating a medication list that seems to stretch endlessly. The constant hum of machines and the beeping of alarms become your new soundtrack. You find yourself immersed in medical jargon you never dreamed you'd understand, emerging as the strongest advocate for your child because, deep down, you know them better than anyone.

Amidst this chaos, however, you discover an unexpected source of hope, strength, and courage. You watch your child confront their illness with remarkable bravery, fighting through harsh treatments while still managing to smile. Their resilience inspires you, igniting a fire within you to keep pushing forward, to fight alongside them. In their moments of strength, you discover your own resilience, even as the weight of despair tries to pull you down.

On days when the journey feels impossible, which it inevitably will, remember to seek out the smallest glimmers of hope. Embrace the beautiful moments amidst the chaos, whether it's a spontaneous dance party in the hospital room to their favourite song, the joy of them finally asking for a favourite snack after days of not eating, or the delight of a new toy from the play staff that brings a brilliant smile. Cherish the comfort of a familiar face visiting or the solace of a chapter from your book paired with a warm cup of tea. It truly is these little things that can make all the difference.

Surround yourself with love and support. Connect with other parents in the ward, join online support groups, and take this journey one step at a time. You are more capable than you realize, and on some days, you may look back in awe at how far you've come. Although this journey will undoubtedly change you, remember that you must keep moving toward those brighter days ahead. You are not alone in this fight, you can and will overcome the challenges that lie ahead.

THE AFTERMATH OF THE STORM —
REMISSION... GETTING ON WITH 'IT'.

"The little reed, bending to the force of the wind, soon

stood upright again when the storm had passed over."

Aesop.

As soon as the battle with cancer officially begins, you are playing a game of snakes and ladders. One minute you are up, the next minute you feel like you are slipping back down. It's a rollercoaster and I promised you that I would tell you the truth. The truth is the battle with cancer is never really over. We all see the adverts on the tv where someone turns to

124

another and says "it's gone" with tears and relief. This portrayal of the end of the battle is what keeps us going during the dark times. However, I hate to be the one to break it to you, this isn't something that will come straight away. Once your child has completed their treatment, you will be told something similar to what we were told when we asked, "what's next?" … the response was "you get on with your lives." This might be something you long for every single day throughout the course of your child's treatment. The thing is, the word 'remission' and the fact that it is depicted in the media as the end of a long, hard, traumatic battle, its actually an illusion. Don't fall into the trap of thinking that once you hear that word that it's all over. Don't fall into a false sense of security, you're not out of the woods yet. Your child will have regular scans for a significant period of time. For my child, I longed for the word 'remission', it was the light at the end of a really dark, terrifying tunnel. However, being told that he would receive quarterly scans for the next five years, it was then that I knew the word 'remission' would never come, not in the way that the media portrayed it.

Another thing that isn't factored in is how it's almost like you've been an elastic band, stretched beyond your limits for a significant period of time, and now they expect you to just snap back to how you were in the beginning, and it will feel impossible. You have spent so much time building up coping strategies and ways of keeping yourself going throughout it all, and now... now what? I remember hearing the words and thinking "how do I do that?" Your life has been on pause for so long and you are just expected to press play like nothing has happened. Be prepared for feeling unprepared and for feeling lost. There is no easy fix for this but in time you will adjust in the same way that you adjusted to having a child who's battling cancer. It's more of a gradual process. Day by day, as time slips by, you will start to feel yourself returning to how things were before this ordeal all started. by this time, you would have got into a rhythm that enables you to cope with the scans and the wait for the results. It will just mean that you function as normal and once a quarter, you will be pulled back to the reality that life is still anything but normal for you. However, once you are enrolled in the cancer club, it's a lifetime membership. There is always going to be a part of you that is looking over your shoulder, waiting to see it cancer wants a rematch. I know this is a difficult pill to swallow, but I promise you do get used to it. You learn to live with that reality. I have been in this situation, and not only did I survive, but I also came out swinging. If I can do it, so can you!

For us, it involved booking a holiday. It was during a trip to Orlando, Florida that I noticed my gut was right and my son was really poorly.

So, when we heard that we needed to get on with our lives, I decided to rebook a trip for the following summer. I checked with the oncologist, and he was completely fine with it. I felt that because the last two years had been filled with negative things, it was time to change the narrative and create some positive ones instead. There was only one problem, four months after booking it, my child relapsed and this time the prognosis wasn't good at all. So, we had a decision to make, cancel or see how the remaining time panned out. I picked the latter. As time went by and my child continued to remain stable, I didn't regret my decision. Until I had to look for travel insurance and contact the airline regarding his travel. There are many different travel insurance companies that I was given by our cancer nurses, and I spent months trying to get my child insured. I had given up at one point and began to email cancer charities to see if they could help.

Then one day, I went back and checked the last few companies on the list I was given. I'll skip to the end, we got insurance, got my child cleared as fit to fly and the holiday was an amazing success with more positive memories than I can possibly recall. However, the point of this is to prepare you for the knock backs you will get from travel insurance companies, the feeling of never catching a break and the fact you might just have to consider selling one of your kidneys to afford the premium.

Then there will be forms sent to you by the airline that you will need to give to your oncologist to complete and return, on several occasions. But if you keep the reason why you are doing it in your head, then you will remain determined to get your family on that plane and to wherever it is you are going. My reasoning was that all three of my children have had a rough time throughout this, they have seen their brother suffer at the hands of cancer for too long and it was time to help them make some positive memories to hold on to. Remission is not a straightforward cut and dried scenario like it is when you have the flu. My advice, keep in mind that the way that remission is depicted as the end of a journey isn't strictly true. Remission represents the end of a chapter and the beginning of a new one. Life won't be the same as it was before your child was diagnosed, but that isn't a bad thing. It just means you are on new terrain. It's okay if this terrain feels alien, and it's okay to feel lost because the terrain doesn't look the way you imagined it would. It's alright if you suffer from the same scanxiety that I do, or if you are daunted by the prospect of trying to be normal after a significant period of time feeling anything but. However, if you don't hold onto anything else, hold onto this, you have survived every storm that cancer has sent your way, your child is still here, and you got through it all. Now? Just like a natural disaster leaves an area completely devastated, you can either mourn what was before, or you can roll up your sleeves and decide what you are going to build on the ruins. You are a warrior, who has walked through fire and come out the other side. No matter what cancer tries to send your way now… you're ready for it. You may not feel like you are ready to trust the calm now that the storm has passed but look up – the light of the lighthouse is still shining, as steady as it has always been.

THE BEACON OF LIGHT — CANCER CHARITIES AND SUPPORT; IT'S OKAY TO ASK FOR HELP.

"You can learn to prevent a storm, or you can learn to ride the storm. If you learn to ride the storm, the storm isn't a problem anymore."

Jaggi Vasudev

In the book "The Boy, The Mole, The Fox and The Horse" by Charlie Mackesy, the boy asks, "What is the bravest thing you have ever said?" and the horse replies "Help". The continued social perception of asking for help as a sign of weakness remains a frustrating fact of life for me.

The reality is that everyone needs help sometimes. However, I think you have gathered by now that when cancer makes an unwelcome appearance, all bets are off. So, I have collated a list of charities and organisations below that may be able to offer financial, emotional, and practical support to you and your family. I have also included the list of travel insurance companies that I scoured through a year ago trying to get my child insured for our trip. I am sure that there are countless more companies that are in the UK right now and ready to help support you in any way that they can. However, these are just a few that I have come across over my child's cancer battle. It is my hope that not only will this book be a lighthouse for you, a fixed point of reference to reach for when the path seems dark and you don't know what lies ahead, but I hope the charities below will be lighthouses for you too.

Financial Assistance

1.   Family Fund

The UK's largest charity providing grants to low-income families raising disabled or seriously ill children. Grants can cover essential items such as household appliances, sensory toys, family breaks and more.

-     Website: https://www.familyfund.org.uk

- Contact: Applications can be made directly through their website.

2. Young Lives vs Cancer

Offers financial support to families, including grants to help with the unexpected costs that cancer brings, such as travel and accommodation near hospitals.

- Website: https://www.younglivesvscancer.org.uk/what-we-do/financialsupport/

- Contact: Reach out via their website for assistance.

3. Macmillan Cancer Support

Provides guidance on accessing various benefits and financial aid, helping families navigate the complexities of the welfare system.

- Website: https://www.macmillan.org.uk/cancerinformationandsupport/impacts-of-cancer/benefitsand-financial-support

- Contact: call 0808 808 00 00 for personalised advice.

4. Lennox Children's Cancer Fund.

Offers practical, financial and emotional support to families

affected by childhood cancer, including respite breaks and

financial grants.

-   Website:

    https://www.childrenwithcancer.org.uk/childhood-

    cancer-info/coping-with-cancer/help-and-support/

-   Contact: Information available directly through their

    website.

Emotional Support.

1. Hope Support Services

Supports children and young people when a close family member

is diagnosed with a serious illness like cancer. They offer a free,

safe online service, including a peer support community.

-   Website: https://www.hopesupport.org.uk
-   Contact: Email – help@hopesupportservices.org.uk or

    call 01989 566317

2. Young Lives vs Cancer – Digital Support Groups Provides

    various digital support programs and workshops for parents

and carers, focusing on key topics and offering a platform to connect

with others in similar situations.

- Website:

    https://www.younglivesvscancer.org.uk/cancer-info-support/body-and-health/online-support-groups/

- Contact: Sign up through their website to join sessions.

3. Macmillan Cancer Support

Offers emotional support for family and friends, providing guidance on coping with a loved one's cancer diagnosis and practical advice for supporting them.

- Website:

    https://www.macmillan.org.uk/cancerinformationandsupport/supporting-someone/emotional-support-for-family-and-friends

- Contact: Call 0808 808 00 00 for support.

4. Childhood Cancer Parents Alliance (CCPA).
Provides practical and emotional support to families, offering information and connecting them with relevant services and

support networks.

- Website:
  https://www.ccpa.org.uk/information/practical-emotional-support/

- Contact: Details available on their website.

5. Molly Olly's Wishes

A UK-based charity that supports children with life-threatening and terminal illnesses, particularly childhood cancer. Founded in memory of Molly Ollerenshaw, who passed away from a rare kidney cancer at age 8, the charity aims to bring comfort to children and their families during difficult times.

- Website: https://www.mollyolly.co.uk

- Contact Details: 01926 698735

Practical Support.

1. Rainbow Trust

Provides emotional and practical support to families who have a child with a life-threatening or terminal illness through dedicated support workers.

- Website: https://www.rainbowtrust.org.uk
- Contact: Information available through their website.

2. Together for short lives.

Offers support for families with children who have life-limiting illnesses, including a helpline and legal advice service. - Website: https://www.togetherforshortlives.org.uk

- Contact: Details available on their website.

3. Solving Kids' Cancer

Provides support to families throughout their child's cancer journey, including financial assistance and post-treatment support programs aimed at enhancing well-being.

- Website: https://solvingkidscancer.org.uk
- Contact: Reach out via their website for more information.

4. Children with Cancer UK

Funds a range of projects to ease the burdens of childhood cancer

diagnosis, including financial hardship grants, free

accommodation

near hospitals, and support programs.

- Website: https://www.childrenwithcancer.org.uk/about-us/what-we-do/wellbeing-and-support/

- Contact: Information available through their website.

Other Lighthouses.

1. Amanda Rose Ferraro

Amanda is a two-time AML Leukaemia Survivor. She is

dedicated to bringing awareness surrounding all aspects of

the AYA cancer journey, including survivorship.

Amanda has a published abstract in the Research Journal of

Oncology, she is a TEDx speaker, she has rallied on Capitol

Hill for legislation that helps cancer patients, and she is a

passionate patient advocate as well as a keynote speaker.

You can find out more about Amanda on her website:
https://cancerisanasshole.com

2. Sharon - @The_Cancer_Mum_Cheerleader

Sharon is a mum of two and a cancer survivor. She is on a mission to spread awareness by squashing the taboo that is around talking about cancer, to ensure that people actually understand that cancer can happen at any time and early detection can save lives.

She can be found on TikTok and Instagram:

@The_Cancer_Mum_Cheerleader

The link to her e-book can be found on her Instagram profile page and you can find her 'Unbreakable Voices' Podcast series on her YouTube Channel

@The_Cancer_Mum_Cheerleader

3. Tim Sadler

Tim is dad to Michael, who was diagnosed in 2014 with Acute Lymphoblastic Leukaemia. He has started a Facebook Group for other dads of children battling cancer.

You can find Mind the Chaps here:

https://www.facebook.com/groups/mindthechaps/?locale=en_GB

Travel Insurance Companies.

Association of British Travel Insurers
0207 600 3333

Able 2 Travel
0189 283 9501

All Clear Travel Insurance
0800 281 3056

Kids Cancer Charity (formerly Christian Lewis)
0179 248 0500

Citybond Sure Travel
0333 207 0506

Freedom Insurance Services
0122 344 6914

Free Spirit Travel Insurance
0800 170 7704

Higos Insurance
0174 683 4500

Insurance Choice
0800 668 0507

Insure and Go
0330 400 1383

InsureCancer (Medi TravelCover Ltd)
0125 278 0190

JD Travel Insurance Consultants
0344 247 4749

Leisure Care
0170 242 7161

Pulse Insurance
0128 084 1430

Staysure
0800 168 8647

The Insurance Surgery (To compare Insurance)
0800 458 0487

World First
0345 908 0161

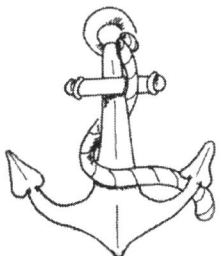

CLOSING STATEMENT BY DR. ANISHA PATEL, GP

As you reach the final pages of this book, I want to take a moment to acknowledge the weight of the journey you have been on. Whether you are reading this as a parent, a carer, a friend, or simply someone seeking understanding, know that every step you have taken, every tear shed, every sleepless night, every act of love has mattered. Cancer is relentless. It does not come with a rulebook, and it does not play fair. But neither does hope. Hope finds its way through the cracks, through the small moments of joy in the darkness, through the kindness of a stranger, through the unwavering resilience of a child. If there is one thing, I want to leave you with, it is this: you are not alone.

And Claire and all the other contributors in this book both patients and practitioners are testament to that – thank you all for sharing your experience that shines light for others. There is strength in shared experiences, in community, in knowing that even when you feel isolated, there are people who understand.

As a doctor, I have seen first-hand how medical advances continue to push the boundaries of what is possible. But I also know that medicine alone not enough. Love, support, holistic care, and self-compassion are just as vital. Give yourself permission to grieve, to feel exhausted, to laugh when you can, and to hold onto whatever anchors you in the storm.

Most importantly, know that your feelings, however messy, however complicated, are valid. Whether you are navigating treatment, remission, or the painful reality of loss, there is no right way to cope.

There is only the next step forward, and then the next.

You have been a lighthouse for your child, for your family, and for yourself. And even when the waters feel rough, your light still shines.

With compassion and solidarity,

Dr Anisha Patel (@doctorsgetcancertoo)

AUTHORS NOTE.

When I began writing this book, I intended to cover all aspects of supporting a child through their battle against cancer. But as the writing progressed, I realised that some parts of this journey are too vast and too profound the confined to a single chapter.

There is a place our minds go when we first hear the diagnosis, and we spend the rest of the journey trying not to revisit it. As a family, we have not heard the word 'terminal' yet, but we are all too aware that it's only a matter of time. The experience of receiving such devastating news, and the unimaginable grief of losing a child, deserves its own space – something that can truly reflect the depth of the heartbreak, the everlasting love, and the courage shown by those who have walked this path before me.

If this is your story, if you have found the courage to keep going when everything inside you feels broken beyond repair, I want you to know that I see you. I hope to honour your strength and your love by telling your story. Because one day, it will be my story too.

You are not alone in this storm.

Claire Pepper

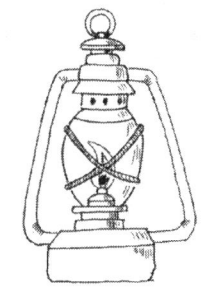

SPECIAL THANKS

This book was born from a feeling of isolation and exhaustion. I often liken it to the portal scene in Avengers: End Game. I was Captain America – holding the line, day in and day out. Exhausted, but immovable. The idea for this book came from seeing that same weary yet determined look in the eyes of other parents in oncology wards and waiting rooms and knowing that something needed to change.

Over time, this book has evolved into a platform with a series of "portals" – avenues of support – just like the moment help arrives for Cap. That look on his face when he realised that he's no longer alone?

That's what I hope to offer others through these pages.

To Jacob, when I told you I wanted to finish the book I had started writing at the beginning of his cancer journey, I expected you to roll your eyes and let me get on with it. Instead, you've been my creative director from the start. I always say I built the lighthouse, but you are the beacon. Your courage, determination, and refusal to be defined by cancer have been woven into every illustration, every page, and every word. You're not a hero or a warrior – you're my boy. You are a fine young man, and I am lucky to be the one you call mum. Cancer can never take that from us. Ever.

To my daughter, thank you for enduring my ineptitude for technology, every Sunday morning idea session over coffee, and for grounding me with a sharp dose of reality (and a side order of teenage sass) when I'm struggling with social media. You are my best friend, and cancer brought us closer together in a way I will always be grateful for. To my husband, thank you for keeping our boat in peak condition – for managing the housework, the school runs, the pastoral parenting, and for being there during the late-night meltdowns when I couldn't get what was in my head onto the page. I couldn't have come this far without you.

To my friends, for offering a lift to the station, opportunities to feel normal, being genuinely interested in how I was doing, and putting up with my insanely dark, chaotic, and inappropriate sense of humour, thank you. I still know who I am thanks to you.

To Tim and Dr Anisha Patel, for writing such a beautiful and honest foreword and closing statement, I am honoured to have fellow lighthouses such as yourselves in the book, shining a guiding light for others who are still weathering their own storms.

Finally, and most importantly, to the parents, children, and medical professionals who entrusted me with their stories ... thank you. What began as one voice has now grown into a chorus that offer others a light in the darkest time of their lives. I could never have done this by myself, and it's been a privilege to share this journey with you.

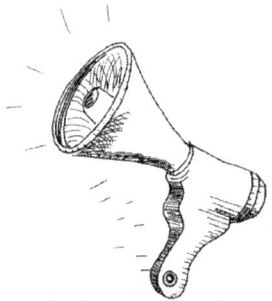

JOIN THE CONVERSATION

What started as a book has grown into a passion for creating a space where all those affected by a child in their family battling cancer can feel seen, heard, understood, and validated. A place where you don't have to choose between being a victim who has pity imposed upon them by others or a being patronised a by being called a warrior and told to "stay strong!".

I want to create a community based on all feelings and emotions being valid all of the time; the good, the bad and the downright ugly. So, if you have felt seen, heard, or understood of within any of the pages of this book, I would like to invite you to join me in keeping this conversation going. Use the hashtag #weatheringcancersstorm and join me in the mission to make sure that no person in this fight feels like they need to pretend or feel like they are alone.

You can find us on:

YouTube at: https://www.youtube.com/@Weatheringcancersstorm

TikTok and Instagram: @weatheringcancersstorm

Podcast: Weathering the Storm of Childhood Cancer - https://open.spotify.com/show/3QtLIAC4BRzUU7LSLm8Nvw?si= WmK4_T1VTnC4wLZUfgttqQ

Website: www.weatheringcancersstorm.com

You can reach us at: claire@weatheringcancersstorm.com

You're doing better than you think.

Printed in Dunstable, United Kingdom

71838259R00086